From "Hard Knocks," by Col. Harry Young.

MISS MARTHA JANE CANARY
In the Melodramatic Rôle of Calamity Jane

Calamity Jane

and the Lady Wildcats

by Duncan Aikman

Introduction by
Watson Parker
with
"Life and Adventures of
Calamity Jane"
by Herself

University of Nebraska Press
Lincoln and London

First Bison Book printing: 1987
Most recent printing indicated by the first digit below:
4   5   6   7   8   9   10

Library of Congress Cataloging-in-Publication Data

Aikman, Duncan, 1889–
  Calamity Jane and the lady wildcats.

  Reprint. Originally published: New York: H. Holt,
c1927.
  1. Cowgirls—West (U.S.)—Biography. 2. Women
pioneers—West (U.S.)—Biography. 3. Jane, Calamity,
1852–1903. 4. West (U.S.)—Biography. 5. West (U.S.)—
Social life and customs. 6. Frontier and pioneer life—
West (U.S.) I. Jane, Calamity, 1852–1903. Life and
adventures of Calamity Jane. 1987. II. Title.
F596.A36   1987   978'.02'0922 [B]   86-25022
ISBN 0-8032-1020-5
ISBN 0-8032-5911-5 (pbk.)

Reprinted by arrangement with Lonnelle Davison Aikman

Dedicated
with some hesitation and
infinite deference
to various
uncontrollable ladies

TABLE OF CONTENTS

LIST OF ILLUSTRATIONS

INTRODUCTION
By Watson Parker

The 1920s were a period of post–World War I female freedom, of an ongoing reaction against the slowly departing Victorianism of the previous generation, and of an outpouring of still guilty Freudian (as it was then understood) sexual unconventionality. Many of the wildcats described here were, I suppose, looked upon in the 1920s as mileposts, or exemplars, or epitomes of what we would today, in the 1980s, call "woman's liberation," but that would be to give them more credit than they deserve. Their lives were not free and easy, but painful and shabby; their conduct was not unconventional so much as uncontrolled. Still, the same fascination that made them interesting to the readers of the 1920s makes them equally interesting to the readers of today. If they weren't the wild, free, and untrammeled spirits as portrayed tongue-in-cheek by Aikman, they should have been, and it is still fun to read about them. Misbehavior has nowadays become so much the norm that it is pleasant to read of times when it was shocking.

Duncan Aikman was born in Terre Haute, Indiana, in 1889. His books include *The Taming of the Frontier* in 1925, a collection of essays by various authors that he assembled and edited. In 1927 he published the present work, for which he is best remembered. In 1926 he published *The Home Town Mind,* in 1940 *All-American Front,* and in 1948 *Turning Stream.* He died on 14 December 1955.

The heft of *Calamity Jane and the Lady Wildcats* deals, as its title implies, with Marthy E. "Calamity Jane" Cannary Burke, who is certainly the best known and most interesting of the lot. Aikman and most others who write about her spell her name Canary, with one *n,* possibly from some notion that she was a sort of songbird of the prairies, but she herself spelt it with two, although her spelling is likely not more reliable, here, than any of her other recollections. This gamey old bawd infested the West generally from the early 1870s to 1903, but her principal locale was Deadwood, South Dakota, and its surrounding mining camps, an area that "would publicize Typhoid Mary as Florence Nightingale if it would help the tourist trade," as one disgruntled South Dakota governor pithily put it when he refused to endorse a movie dealing with a rejuvenated and sanitized but still notorious old Calam'.

Even in her prime Calamity looked like a busted bale of hay and was the roughest looking human being the miners participating in the Black Hills gold rush had seen. She was drunk most of the time, and noisily drunk, a defect of character that stayed with her till she died. Whether she was libidinous because of a natural or cultivated inclination, or because she was usually so drunk she couldn't put up much resistance, or because she needed the money for liquor is not easy to say; likely all those factors contributed to her not so much lustful as abandoned behavior. She had her good side, and she is said to have nursed smallpox victims in the Deadwood pesthouse (the epidemic was both brief and mild), but if she did it is likely that she gave the ambulatory and convalescent sufferers the great pox or some other bane in exchange, for nobody can be long in the prostitution business and not have more than transient joy to pass along to her consumers. Indeed, it seems likely to me, a cynical old army medic, that this may well have been the source of her name: her paramours were likely to suffer from some venereal calamity.

But she was generous, with everything she had. She stole from a customer in a whorehouse to help pay the medical bills of one of the other girls. In her later years she became sort of a joke in Deadwood, cadging, bullying, and stealing, largely on her own account but now and then to further some passing charitable instinct. She bought two huge sacks of candy for Judge Bennett's daughter and her chum—or, rather, ordered grocer Goldberg to charge them up to her account, which never did get paid. A Mrs. Drowly of Glendive, Montana, wrote in the margin of Estelline Bennett's chapter on Calamity Jane in *Old Deadwood*

Days (UNP, 1982), that she could "vouch for the fact that she loved children. My mother tells me when I was very young she left me with my brother. I put my finger in an old pump and my brother proceeded to pump, breaking my finger. When mother came home Calamity Jane was walking the floor with me and singing 'Hot Time in the Old Town Tonight.'" She was like that: generous when she was sober, which wasn't very often.

After a while the joke wore thin. The editor of the *Deadwood Champion* mused, in her own day, that "as far as real merit is concerned, she is a fraud and a dead giveaway. A hundred waiter girls or mop squeezers in this gulch are her superiors in everything; her form and figure are not only indifferent but repulsive. It makes me tired to see so much written about such a woman." Old "Judge" Kuykendall, who earned his title by presiding over the initial miners' trial of Jack McCall for the murder of Wild Bill Hickok, wrote with feeling in his declining years that "charity dictates that the veil of oblivion should be drawn over the character of that woman."

Well, the veil of oblivion wasn't drawn. Oblivion was just what these wildcats didn't want; they wanted publicity, notoriety, and the center front on the stage of life in the drama of the West. There were a lot more worthy women on the frontier, women who didn't advertise, took a back seat, did their work and kept quiet, but their lives, truthfully told, are generally not as interesting to read about as are the doddering fabrications of these gaudy old gaswells who sought publicity, good or bad, wherever they could find it. Madam Moustache, for example, was short, pudgy, and notably unattractive for the major part of her existence. If she had charm, it soon faded into acumen, and like most successful gamblers she succeeded mainly by staying sober and not playing against other professionals. Belle Starr, her photographs show, was afflicted with plainness as if with a disease, and one look at her pictures pretty well washes out any notion of romance in *her* existence. Lola Montez started out as the mistress of a crazy king, and went downhill from there, steadily. And so it went for most of them: the primrose path in actual practice was a pretty lumpy highway, with more thorns than roses along the way, and those who trod it for a living did not have much free time to pause to pick the posies.

It follows from the nature of Aikman's subjects that if he had stuck entirely to known and demonstrable truths about them his book wouldn't have been much more than a pamphlet. He had to take what information, good or bad, true or doubtful, came to hand, and even doing so he probably had to do some faking in addition. He relies heavily upon Calamity Jane's own *Life and Adventures,* which because of its rarity and interest has been added here. It was probably ghostwritten in the early 1890s, and it is so full of errors that when it is correct it is only so by accident. To the extent that Aikman depended upon it, he is likely to be mistaken as to his facts and any conclusions that he draws from them. Ramon Adams, in his cantankerous *Burrs under the Saddle* points this out, and goes on to discredit much of what Aikman wrote about Belle Starr, claiming that much of his research likely depended upon old files of the *Police Gazette,* that fertile incubator of criminological error and exaggeration. Time after time, says Adams, Aikman puts Belle in the wrong place, at the wrong time, and for the wrong reason. But let us face it: the wildcats would have loved it; *this* is just the kind of publicity that they sought and wanted, and accuracy be damned. In their own way, they were geniuses at public relations, especially as they got older, and certainly Aikman has written of them in a way that they would have enjoyed and that we can, taken with a sack of salt to the chapter, enjoy today.

For those particularly interested in old Calam' — and I judge that these will constitute the bulk of the readers of this book — J. Leonard Jennewein's *Calamity Jane of the Western Trails* (Huron, S.D.: Dakota Books, 1953) and Roberta B. Sollid's *Calamity Jane — A Study in Historical Criticism* (Helena: Montana Historical Society, 1958) are likely to be the most useful books. Both question that she was ever married to Wild Bill Hickok, as does Joseph E. Rosa's masterful study of that turbulent but fastidious gunfighter, *They Called Him Wild Bill* (Norman: University of Oklahoma Press, 1964).

FOREWORD

I AM indebted to a great many individuals for making the collection of the material for these sketches possible and agreeable.

Mr. Charles I. Mullinax, town historian and police judge of Princeton, Mo., was indefatigable in searching for records and recollections of the stay of Martha Jane Canary and her parents in Princeton, and I was greatly assisted in tracing the family's Missouri career by the vivid memory of Mrs. Elizabeth Collins.

In the Black Hills invaluable sources of information were found for me by Mr. Duncan Elder of the Deadwood *Pioneer-Times*. I am indebted for essential material on Calamity Jane and the "days of '76" to M. J. Russell, J. S. McClintock and Percy Russell of Deadwood; to Peter A. Gushurst of Lead; to Richard B. Hughes of Rapid City; and to Jesse W. Brown of Sturgis, both for private recollections and for permission to use Brown and Willard's "Black Hills Trails" as source material.

In Wyoming Mr. Alfred J. Mokler of

Casper generously allowed me to use his invaluable "History of Natrona County" as a basis for my account of Cattle Kate and also assisted with the results of his unpublished research on her career. Mrs. Cyrus Beard and Miss Eunice C. Hastie of the Wyoming Department of History contributed significantly to this subject in the way of contemporary records. Dr. Grace Raymond Hebard of the Department of Political Economy and Sociology in the University of Wyoming at Laramie furnished numerous helpful suggestions and at the sacrifice of much time arranged two essential interviews on Calamity Jane and Madame Moustache with Mr. Charles W. Bocker of Laramie.

Mr. George E. Abbott of Cheyenne made possible many pleasant contacts with Wyoming old-timers, and to John M. Hunton, Esq., of Torrington, Wyoming, I am indebted for much background information on plains and military life of Calamity Jane's time and for important data on Calamity herself. Mr. Howard F. Vickery of the Sheridan, Wyoming, *Post-Enterprise* helped me to unearth valuable incidental material on Calamity Jane in northern Wyoming.

In Montana Mr. David Hilger and his staff at the State Historical Library made possible a helpful study of social conditions in the Alder Gulch camps during Calamity Jane's adolescence there, and Mr. P. T. Tucker of Livingston contributed useful recollections of Calamity's Kansas phase. Thomas Beer, author of "The Mauve Decade," also supplied a number of important Calamity anecdotes from the family memorabilia of the west. Two old soldiers of the Indian wars who furnished me with much forcefully debunking information about Miss Canary's "military" career are Malecki W. Dillon of Denver and Charles Angus of Livingston.

For invaluable research assistance I am indebted to Miss Margaret Hart, librarian of the San Francisco *Bulletin*, on Lola Montez; to Dean Collins of the Portland, Oregon, *Telegram* on Bridget Grant; and to Miss Effie R. Keen, secretary to the Arizona State Historian, on "The Last Lady Road Agent." Mr. Boutwell Dunlap of San Francisco has been unfailingly helpful in advice and information out of his expert knowledge of early California history. Mr. E. A. Brininstool of Los Angeles put his western collections and his wide acquaintance with western lore and history at my disposal to my great profit. Idwal Jones of the San Francisco *Examiner* materially assisted my sophistication with the scrap books of his newspaper writings on early San Francisco celebrities, morals and customs.

I have drawn liberally on S. W. Harman's "Hell on the Border," Phœnix Publishing Company, Fort Smith, Arkansas, for material on Belle Starr. I have also had helpful criticism on the Belle Starr manuscript from John H. McGinnis, professor of English in Southern Methodist University and literary editor of the Dallas *News*, some of which unfortunately came too late to be incorporated in the article. Judge Llewellyn H. Davis and Hamilton W. Rayner of El Paso have supplied agreeable anecdotal material.

To many others who have helped with useful suggestions and valuable information about the individual "lady wildcats" and their environment, I offer thanks no less personal for being generally expressed.

D. A.

CALAMITY JANE
AND THE LADY WILDCATS

CALAMITY JANE

A SLIGHT little girl in torn pinafore and auburn hair shaken wildly out of its braids danced about over a thicket of fallen logs in the woods of northern Missouri. The September sun limbered her muscles warmly for violent exercise. The September gale was cool enough to hold off fatigue forever. With the gusts a checkered shade of thinning leaves hurled itself tö and fro in the bright ravine, syncopations of a jazz played by sunlight.

Jerking to its formless tempo, the little girl flung her arms about like the young saplings, ducked her head backward and forward, twisted her slim body in startling curves and angles. She pranced up and down the big, rough-barked logs with the antic grace of a cake-walker, slipped on their mossy sides, recovered herself in leaps like a young wildcat's. To the springy sapling trunks she clung with wild balancing lunges and the clutch of brown, almost prehensile toes.

The thinking part of her was closed, as if she had forgotten it. Only her body knew, inarticulately, that it was delicious to be eight years old and have perfect command of every limb and muscle. Her clutching toes knew, her taut shoulder tendons, her wildly swaying waist knew that no log or combination of logs, low or high, slippery or with the cutting edge of hacked timber, could trip her. Perfectly supple, she need think of no words, she could express suppleness in motion only. There was no humor, hardly even conscious mirth in her shrieks of ecstatic laughter; only her vocal muscles at play with the rest.

A dozen little boys pelting her with corn-cobs from a near-by clump of bushes could not hit her. Not all her little cousins, the sons of her uncle Thornton Canary, not all their husky playmates from the whole corn-shuck-ing neighborhood, not all the little boys in the world could hit her with a corncob, or hurt her if they did. Her agility, her swiftness, her perfect wind for violent exercise mesmer-ized her into dreamy exaltations of self-confi-dence. She was the soldier who could only be hit with the silver bullet, and there were no silver bullets. She was the invulnerable, the inviolable, the defiant, spirit of September light and air and energy embodied.

Suddenly it came upon her that she must let them know this ecstasy. This little world of bush clumps, fallen logs, yelling small boys, whirring corncobs, pouring sunshine, must be told that she was more than a match for it, and knew it. They must be shamed with your superiority, taunted. To taunt them sufficiently was worth giving all you had.

The little girl gave it. She screeched inarticulate arrogance like a young monkey defying its jungles. It was not enough. They were not impressed enough. They kept on whirling the corncobs. They screeched back.

After all she would have to put it into words.

"Damn your souls to hell," she screamed in joyous tantrum, "if one of them cobs hits me, I'll scratch your —— —— eyes out."

Not much happens in Princeton, Missouri. Incredibly old Civil War veterans sit aimlessly about the railway station all summer long. They move with the shade, whittling. They josh each other amiably about prohibition violations which rarely occur and about the imaginary infatuations they have aroused in the haughty young girls who appear at the day coach windows. The middle-aged loll back deep in the cool dark of old-fashioned store buildings, fanning themselves and waiting for customers. Even the younger set date their profoundest social experiences by high school plays and the Methodist lawn socials.

A woman, young or old, cursing publicly is as much of a rarity as a woman tourist smoking a cigarette in the public square.

So they have remembered this of her for sixty-seven years.

Her name was Martha Jane Canary, and I regret to suggest that she came by her language from her mother. There was, for that matter, almost as much title to lasting remembrance in being Charlotte Canary's eldest daughter as in being the little girl who swore.

The county seventy years ago was pioneer farm land. That meant that its "good women" made it a virtue to wear themselves with house-chores, chills and fever, salivations and child-bearing into farm hags as soon as possible after their twentieth birthdays. Charlotte offended by remaining when long past her middle twenties, and the mother of half-grown children, flamboyant, easy to look at, insolently youthful. Turbulent coppery-red hair tumbled loosely from under her modish store bonnets, when by rights of her age and social condition it should have been thin and stringy and entirely hidden under a sun-bonnet. The local mode in cheeks tended toward a sunken sallowness. Charlotte's were plump, clear, highcolored and just a trifle, but most seductively, freckled. A practiced boldness in her large brown eyes challenged men when it was a well-established convention that farm wives, in public, should look sullenly groundward as though deploring original sin, hard work and cumulative evidence that the woman pays.

Charlotte kept, too, a lithe but interestingly luxuriant figure. Worse, by the most reliable recollections of both sexes, she consciously postured it as she galloped her horse a bit too noisily back and forth along the road between Princeton and the Canary farm at the Collins church settlement, or walked about on her notoriously frequent errands in the Princeton public square. Even at her house-keeping, which she performed with a speed and efficiency especially annoying to her numerous enemies, she eschewed the traditional sacking and printless cotton for gaudier colors and

softer fabrics.   On her Princeton appearances
her costume was generally considered brazen.
Hence, few of the idle or employed gentry of
Mercer county let her pass without turning
their glances on her in guarded animation and
tongues were not lacking to charge that some
who turned knew when and where to follow.

In a word, Charlotte was an early Missouri
exotic.   The community could understand
Princeton's two or three notorious and definitely slatternly women of the town.   It could
find a place in its social hierarchy for a few
comely but unwashed wives or the poor white
trash element on the hard-scrabble hill farms
who bore children now and then to the elegant
gentry of Mercer county's half a dozen southern manorial estates and wantonly christened
the offspring with the family names of their
fathers to testify the honor that had been done
them.   But it could not understand a beautiful, coarse woman who smoked, drank, cursed
and publicly flirted, yet refused to be caught
in *flagrante delicto*.   Charlotte flaunted the
conventions both of local respectability and its
opposite.   The community repaid her by be-
stowing upon her the thing she no doubt most
ardently desired of it, its notice.

With horror or humor according to its mood, it delighted to circulate the scandal, said to be on the authority of her own brother-in-law's wife, the eminently normal farm mother, Mrs. Thornton Canary. By this sisterly version, Bob Canary, an innocent and not too shrewd young farm boy, had been bedazzled by Charlotte's beauty in her early teens when he had found her in an Ohio bawdy house. On the spot he had married her to reform her. He was not, it would be said with snickering shudders, after ten years, making too successful a job of it.

But it was even pleasanter to get down to certified local data: the piratical obscenities with which the neighbors, aroused in their beds by the shrill tones coming across the cornfields on still summer nights, had heard her "cussing out" Bob for not being a more successful agriculturist; the delicate terminology she had used, on one of her more than usually raucous visits, in telling the general storekeeper, the postmaster, the town constable and possibly the saloon-keeper their shortcomings. It became, in fact, one of the recognized social relaxations among the less prim sets of Mercer county to argue how full Charlotte had got on her last public appearance.

One of these instances has come down after sixty-six years, not entirely to her discredit. During a January thaw the winter after the Civil War opened, Charlotte came riding in a splatter of muck and enthusiasm out from Princeton on the Collins church road. The military mode had evidently got into her consciousness for straight above her shoulder she carried a long pole with a wide spread of calico attached like a trooper's battle flag. Like a trooper, too, she stopped and stood at salute at the door of the fifteen-year-old bride who lived on the next farm to hers in the double embarrassment of extreme poverty and a young baby.

The reputation of Charlotte on her rampages was anything but soothing and the girl appeared on her threshold hardly in the mood of a perfect hostess. Charlotte eyed her for a moment with the glassy exultation of inebriate play-acting. Then, violently but deftly, she tossed the flag-pole, calico and all, at the young mother's feet.

"Hey," she said genially, "take that and

make a dress for your damn bastard." And
with another splatter of mud and a cavalryman's oath to her old gray horse was gone.

Calico was at the fabulous summit of cotton
blockade prices. The young mother swallowed
rancor and shocked proprieties and carried her
gift into the house.

Still, when you were a little girl of eight or
nine and liked to dash about on tall gray horses,
dance like a squirrel over log thickets and swear
at the boys harder than they dared swear at each
other, it must have been exhilarating to have a
mother who could do all these and so many
others, even better than you. It must have
been agreeable not to be restrained from raiding the sugar barrel, tantrums, staying up at all
hours, roaming the woods and bottom lands
like an Indian and going swimming in the
creeks when you felt like it, because for less
privileged little girls such conduct wasn't considered "nice."

It must have been exciting to have a mother
whom you could rely on for treats and presents
from town at the most unexpected hours and
who could almost always be trusted, if whippings were in the atmosphere, to try out her

skill on somebody her own size instead of on you, on your mild and scarcely noticeable father, for instance.

Even at ten years, it must have given a thrill to be known as the child of the town "wildcat," to feel that you had such a gaudy reputation to sustain for colorfully outrageous conduct.

But the bold brown eyes which challenged men also scorned homelier and harder-working women in a way that made them vixenishly conscious of their superior virtue, whether over the "wildcat" or the "wildcat's" kitten. However Charlotte's examples and Bob's supine timidity affected her, Charlotte's child would never have her morals corrected by whiningly virtuous strangers as sometimes happened to the little girls of the apathetic poor white trash women when the evangelical ladies' aid societies were on the prowl. Charlotte's reputation, Charlotte's fighting spirit warned them off. And now that she was old enough to cuss out the boys and not get hit by corncobs, so did Charlotte's child.

Rather than take anything off these psalm-singing old fun-spoilers, she, like her mother, would grow up to be the toast of half the bar-rooms, the dance houses, the Indian-fighting

regiments from Walla Walla to Dodge City;
from Hell on Wheels to Asbestos, as one of her
admirers of the old west delicately puts it.
Rather than that she'd become Calamity Jane;
and she did.

A good deal of Princeton, apart from her
mother's stimulating companionship, went into
her making.   Yet no one can even be sure when
she came there.   Forty years after, she herself
was to declare that the town was her birthplace.
But did she know?   She was furnishing
material for an autobiography which, judging
by its exaggerations elsewhere, she took with
enormous seriousness.   A story of anybody's
life,—hell, it had to begin with a birthplace.
She knew that much, or if she did not, the
smart young fellow who was writing it down
just as he prompted her to dictate it, knew it.
So if in a life of wandering, confusion, excitement and more or less constant potations,
she had forgotten where she was born, or if
Charlotte in her hectic concern with more
entertaining adventures had neglected to mention it, Princeton, anyhow, was the first place
she remembered.   So Princeton it was.   And
since her birthday was the first of May and

she remembered having heard something about the year 1851 or 1852, she'd begin, "I was born in Princeton, Missouri, May 1, 1852," and let it go at that. It was a whole lot nearer the truth, she reminded herself with a possibly beery wink, than some other things in that pamphlet.

But the chances are that she was three or four years old when she came to Princeton and she may have been seven or eight. Her grandfather, James Canary, bought the family's first land-holding, the 280-acre farm in the Collins church district, in May, 1855. It is hardly probable that in that land-hungry time a man with the cash or credit to buy so much acreage in a fertile and fairly populous settlement would have hung around a county for three years either as a farm laborer or as a capitalist awaiting a promising investment. Much more probably Grandfather Canary had sold an unsatisfactory farm up in Iowa near Burlington and moved immediately over the state line into the northern tier of Missouri counties to try another one, timing his arrival as nearly as possible with the planting season. This makes it plausible that the critics of the autobiographical pamphlet are right in claiming that Martha

Jane was born near Burlington, although it would take an opinionated guesser in vital statistics to be sure of it.

But did Grandfather Canary bring along Bob and Charlotte, Martha Jane and the other babies? This, I think, is entirely plausible. Princeton's old-timers remember Bob working in the fields with the old man and are pretty sure that the couple was "around" for the better part of ten years. Neither of these impressions would have been probable if Bob had merely dropped in early in October, 1859, when the grandfather was dying, and, as the records show, bought 180 acres of the farm for the rather nominal price of five hundred dollars. His more ambitious brother, Thornton, was in the neighborhood earlier, buying land on a considerable scale on the other side of the county. Bob, with his chronic listlessness, the dependence on family ties which made him put up with a wife who was both a neighborhood scandal and a termagant, was the kind of a man to stick close to a father who had means enough to buy 280 acres. The whole situation suggests that the Canarys conducted their emigrations as a family group until Grandfather Canary died.

So Jane lived probably seven or eight years in Princeton, and certainly more than three. She had her first memories there. What were they?

The county was less than twenty years reclaimed from the Indians. Away from its clearings, it was still virgin forest. When you had a mother who didn't care what you did with your time and made no effort to control you, and a father too worn out from farm work and domestic inferiority to try, you could make much of this. You could scramble about the woods all day after berries. You could borrow one of the farm nags, when they weren't all in use for the plowing and for Charlotte's town errands, and go tearing up to the hill billies' farms for sociability, or plunge through the forests for the sheer fun of motion.

You could sneak an old sawed-off squirrel gun from somewhere—father would never notice and mother wouldn't give a cuss—and spend a cheerful day pot-shooting dangerously at the landscape and rather less effectively at various small varmints. You could run with a pack of snarling, acrobatic, dirty small boys in the nutting and swimming-hole seasons, leaving them to "catch Satan" from their mothers for having you along, but comfortably sure you wouldn't catch it for going. Meanwhile you could learn from them how to handle your body like an infant Amazon, and collect certain charmingly unconventional diversions which were infinitely removed from Scoutcraft. Your poor white friends in the hill farms, too, could acquaint you with interesting, almost awe-inspiring secrets of country depravity and teach you, if Charlotte's example had not already, how to gulp down an occasional thrilling hooker of raw pioneer whiskey without shuddering.

It was an amusing neighborhood, too, you learned as your powers of observation sharpened and you got to know its slapstick back-stairs life. Mother was funny when she came home tight and good-natured to shoot off her harum scarum language, or stage bear dances on the cabin floor to make the children hilarious, or to put on those exciting opera house poses like that of the cavalryman before she shelled out some trifling but delightful gift. Father was funny when he took his cussings out with an occasional half-jocular protest which only made Charlotte cuss harder and which you didn't know—and he didn't know—was properly called irony and was really, under the circumstances, rather pathetic. All this, of course, never for an instant shocked you. It was all you knew in the way of domestic entertainment and you accepted it quite as gratefully as little mid-Victorian girls in richer and more orderly households did when their parents amused them with Christmas charades.

The whole neighborhood, in fact, was full of admirably grotesque characters. There were the men and boys of the poor white trash families who got so blind drunk that their staggerings were as entertaining as circus acrobatics. Yet in this state they would get insanely angry over nothing, itself a charming bit of comedy, and bite, scratch, gouge, wrestle each other until suddenly, all covered with blood and mud, they would make friends again. Their women, with their hair-pullings, garment-rendings and screechings, would put on an even more gorgeous and exciting form of slapstick when their feuds and their liquors moved them. There were the gay young sports from the rich farms and the three or four sure enough brick houses of Princeton, who would come, all in their stylish clothes and their hell-raising mannerisms, to the hill billies' dances, whirl the women wildly off their feet in the tipsy reels, buss them, wrestle with them. They would pull horse pistols excitingly on the men when they became ugly and, when they left, scatter impressive but not really very large collections of bank notes in their wake to pay for damages emotional and sundry.

You knew the gossip, too, as to who Squire Willie So-and-So was "hoppin' around with." In your vague childish way you understood that this was deliciously amusing with a very broad accent. You had known, always, it seemed, that the very apex of comedy was reached when some able-bodied citizen got so drunk that he could no longer keep his eyes open or stand up. So you gave your shrill little-girl's laughter to the jest when the story went around that a waggish customer had come into Tollerday's store, which occasionally sold groceries as well as squirrel whiskey, one day and found six drunks stretched out on the floor in perfect unconsciousness. "Tollerday," the customer had said, "that bacon o' yourn is goin' to spile if I don't immejutly remove it." And one after another he had picked up the drunks to dump them down a chute, feet-first, into the cellar's half-full brine vat.

Perhaps there were only three drunks, or one drunk, instead of six. Perhaps none of it ever happened and the waggish customer simply imported the story from Illinois or Arkansas to get the laugh on Tollerday. But to the little girl of ten whose playground was among the rough small boys and the lewdly obstreperous doings of the off-color group in a pioneer settlement, such sights and such tales were Sunday school picnic, children's vaudeville and movie comic rolled into one. If Martha Jane had known the slang of the 1920's she would have breathed with each new ecstasy of bawdy merriment— "This is the life."

Thus the Princeton years taught her to love the open, uncontrolled state of the houseless and the half-housed who, by their own philosophy and the evidence of all her experience, were the only ones free to enjoy life. She knew instinctively that she must run with men and boys, hard-featured, profane, open-handed and reckless, and with rare women like Charlotte who could enjoy it without qualms. It had dawned on her, as the proprieties dawn upon others, that the stupid, respectable, hard-working farmer-folk of churches and recurrent mortgage worries had not learned the only true art—Charlotte's art—of living life for the last ounce of fun there was in it. Already, for her, all real pleasure must contain a flare of ostentatiously bawdy humor to parody and shock the plodding seriousness of the proper and the tame-minded. Already, she scorned, as beneath all bipeds, the prissily good little girls and the mournfully virtuous women who were not allowed contact with such gayeties or with little girls who had made a contact, because they were not "nice." Princeton had made Martha Jane a small, untutored rebel against the codes, with the creed of "to hell with the consequences" to guide her.

It was going on 1863 and Martha Jane was going on twelve and she heard that the family in the spring would be moving west. In litheness of body and the sophistication she craved, Martha Jane was ready for it.

They went west, no doubt, for obvious reasons and some others. They were a half-nomadic pioneer family, whose moving habit was now, with Martha Jane, getting established in the third generation. They had been in Princeton for nearly eight years, and they were tired of it on general principles. Bob had been

farming on the same spot for eight crop seasons
and was no richer in land or profits than when
he came.

On the other hand, the Civil War was on and
while he was not yet getting appreciably more
for his corn and his oats, he was paying a lot
more for the things Charlotte bought at Princeton's profiteering emporiums.   That fall of
1862 she hurled more picaresque phrases than
usual about his ears for not being a good enough
farmer to keep a wife in the bright colors her
charm   and   her   war   psychosis   demanded.
There were soldiers riding through every week
or so, this being Missouri, and half the strapping young farm boys in the county were in
uniform.

Nor were these economic and possibly erotic
difficulties all of the war's discomforts.   The
county was just over the line from frantically
loyal Iowa.   In the first year, it had turned
violently Unionist and was doing all in the
power of the current Missouri fashions in
opinion compulsion to make things hot for the
southern minority.   Bob and Charlotte may or
may not, so far as the records are available, have
been native Kentuckians, and Bob was mild
and negative enough to have weathered the

storm whether he was or not. But Charlotte, whatever her nativity, was certainly a Kentuckian by reputation and in the neighborhood's opinion of her violent, high-stepping conduct. This went more and more naturally, according to the primly loyal opinion of the Unionist gossips, with being the village wildcat.

So the story started that Charlotte in her cups was getting to be a "secesh spitfire" besides what everybody knew she was. Bob's apathy to all the local patriotic labors from home guard enlistment to loyalist rallies gave color to the scandal. Bob's apathy, to be sure, was too genuine to be pointedly political. He was by now apathetic to practically everything, including Charlotte's public carousals with visiting soldiers. And quite possibly Charlotte's Confederate propaganda was merely a device to shock once more a community which had been shocked already almost out of the habit of noticing her. Nevertheless during 1862 the community's established but half-kindly disapproval of the Collins settlement Canarys deepened into resentment. From being humorously tolerated, they came to be suspected, a little hated. Nothing indicates that they were interfered with, mobbed or even ordered to move on. But in December Bob sold the farm, and after living out the winter on it by some neighborly arrangement, in the spring they moved.

The little bride who had been given the calico on the flag-pole stood at her cabin door and waved them down the road with their covered wagon, two horses, three cows and brace of lean, yellow Missouri hounds. She had helped with the loading up and the house-cleaning. Now she had a whole bed-quilt full of Charlotte's cast-off finery and household gear to remember them by. So she liked Charlotte more than a little, secessionist sentiments, carousals, virago performances and all.

"A crazy, show-off, harum-scarum woman, drunk or sober," she paid her tribute sixty-four years later, "but good-hearted at the core." And little Martha Jane might have a curse of her own and be "wild as a lynx's kitten." But this old neighbor had never seen her indulge in a prank that was worse than any other tomboy's whose parents made no effort to control her, and remembers that she was better than most girls her size with babies.

Anyway, they were off for the next test of

the great illusion. With Bob, it was the hope that somewhere out in Kansas or Nebraska territory, where land cost practically nothing and crops were sure of a soldiers' market, he could make enough to give Charlotte the clothes, the horses, the liquor and the spending money she wanted and somehow shut off her caterwaulings. With Martha Jane it was a dream of living forever among husky frontiersmen who didn't give a damn what your manners or your morals or your living conditions were, so long as you kept moving and had a continuous good time. Charlotte, no doubt, lifting up the jug occasionally as the March sun became luxurious, lay back in the straw and saw visions of other farm land county seats which could be plagued anew by a farm-wife nearing thirty who would yet dare to drink, swear, dress gaudily and be good to look upon; of other cross-roads stores and post-offices whose loungers would react with a flattering sensual attention to a figure consciously postured at the porch posts and the glance of brown eyes that knew how to be bold.

Or was she thinking, with the secret insight of women who know how and when to use their emotional outbursts, of what she could do with Bob for her own long checked amusement now that at last she had got him uprooted?

Whatever she was thinking, the Canarys were through with being rooted to any farm. We know surprisingly little of how it happened, considering that the most celebrated member of the family later dealt in autobiography. Charlotte and Bob told the Mercer County neighbors that they were going out west to take up land in the spring. But a year from the next winter they turn up in Alder Gulch, Montana, plying the least agricultural trades conceivable.

How much Martha Jane understood of this changing decision is questionable. No doubt they plodded on agreeably enough over the greening hills and through the swampy mud of northern Missouri and northeastern Kansas. Bob must have stopped a day or two now and then in attractive localities to chaffer over the price of promising farm sites, and complained querulously that land was higher already than it had been "back east"—100 miles or so!— last year. Charlotte, with such an opening, inevitably cursed him for the fool he was to sell out just before a war market ripened. Then she would freshen herself to go into the little wayside towns and be stared at by new knots of friendly yokels. Martha Jane would borrow one of the nags and go off bare-back to discover the country.

Pushing on at this pace, it would be summer before they could reach the open prairies where the government land was. Did they take up land, anyway, put in a late crop and fail at it? Or did they take their first holiday from farm life and mill around some huge bull train camp like Independence or the new Kansas City? They could have lived by their farm sale proceeds and what Bob could earn driving beef for the armies or freight for the smaller but equally demanding army of prospectors out panning for gold in the creeks around Denver City.

It is all guess-work. They were not the kind of folk to write letters. Even if they had been, the Princeton neighbors, when they left, were hardly in a mood to solicit correspondence. So all we can be sure of is that somewhere on the plains or in the freighting camps in '63 they heard, in a crescendo of enticing details, that the new Montana gold strike was the richest ever made.

It would be like Charlotte to give Bob no peace after that. In the intimacy of a prairie dug-out or a covered wagon, Martha Jane must have learned how domestic destinies can be settled once and for all. All day long and as long as she could stay awake at night she could hear the canvas flapping to the familiar storm of billingsgate.

What sort of a tin-horn husband was this, anyway, who after plugging along at one farm after another all his life and getting nowhere, was afraid to take a chance at a trade where he might make a living fit for a white woman? He didn't know anything about mining? Well, a lot his skill at busting clods and shucking corn had got him in twenty years. Any big stand-up-in-the-corner could dig a hole with a pick and wash pebbles in a dishpan, couldn't he? Was it any harder than selling oats for less than it cost to grow them?

He just naturally wasn't lucky? Wouldn't find any gold? Well, there were plenty of things a smart young fellow could do in a mining camp to make money besides hard work, if that was what he was afraid of. She'd learned a thing or two about card tricks back where he met her. She could teach him how. . . . Anyway, to come right down to it, he could either go on with her to the gold-fields or watch her go on with some fellow who had the guts. If he didn't believe it, just let him remember the way the men made eyes at her in that wagon train that passed them yesterday, —or the day before. . . . And so on.

Until, sooner or later, Bob realized that it was a question of farm work and farm poverty along with Charlotte's bullyings, or of Charlotte's bullyings without farm work and possibly without poverty, too; and chose the lesser evil.

So Charlotte could sit back again and be genial for a whole winter, and between swigs of war time whiskey remind herself of what the hags and hussies of the trail had told her when she met them at the freighting depots: that these mining camps were places where it was worth a fortune simply to have a woman's body. That beat being reformed in the Missouri backwoods, she would inform herself and possibly an admiring if somewhat uncomprehending Martha Jane, with bursts of mildly inebriate laughter. And if Bob Canary didn't like it, he could go jump in the river.

The point had been decided in favor of Martha Jane's advanced education in the science of hard-living, assuming her to have passed the primary course with honors in Mercer county and a highly practical preparatory course in the freighting camps and on the roads. In the spring of '64 they were off to procure, for this precocious and thoroughly ambitious young prodigy, the equivalents of a finishing school.

They took, said her autobiography of thirty-five years later, the Overland route. When the autobiography is both exceptionally matter-of-course and exceptionally plausible, there is no reason for doubting it. The big emigrant trains almost invariably followed the Overland. Shelter and supplies were to be had that way at the Pony Express stations. Relays of military guard would protect them from Indians. The Canarys, evidently from the context, joined a big train, and they would. Bob's self-reliance was hardly equal to tackling a compass-steered course across the Indian-infested prairies direct to Montana even if Charlotte's lack of confidence in his single-handed Indian-fighting qualities would have let him.

This meant that they went in an almost straight line from Independence or some slightly more western outpost to Julesburg, Colorado, and then through Cheyenne, Laramie, the future—and now past—South Pass City on down the Green River valley of Wyoming and Utah into Salt Lake. Then they turned north across the deserts and grotesque barren mountains of northern Utah and southern Idaho up to the Montana gulches.

They were, by the autobiography's account, five months on the way. This was average progress for 2,000 miles through prairie mud and desert where horses must hold in their pace so as not to tire the oxen, and across snow-swollen streams and up delirious passes where the oxen's pace was quite enough. Jane found it wholly stimulating. There were the thirty-foot whips of the bull-whackers to be tried out with the husky young muscles of her twelve-year-old shoulders, and the quite as exhilarating thirty-foot oaths of the bull-whackers as well. There was wilder country to be ridden over than she had ever dreamed of in Missouri, and better, because in the clear, treeless light,

you could see more of it. If she rode at all far
from the train, she must ride with the hunters,
and here was a new kind of man, more after
her own heart than the sottish town hellions of
Princeton; dry, silent, physically self-confident
men with their gorgeous feats of riding and
marksmanship, with exciting lore of varmints,
with snatches of hoarse confidences to be over-
heard by a little girl with quick ears, concerning adventures, none too delicate, in the freighting camps and in squawland.

Here, too, were hair-breadth physical escapades that put corn-cob dodging on a Missouri
log thicket definitely into the class of kinder-
garten gymnastics. There was the day when
they could not get the heavy wagons down the
mountain-side. It took a little girl of slight
weight and limbs sure as a tree monkey's to ease
herself hand over hand up sapling clumps and
find the place where they could anchor the
ropes. There were nights under the moon and
stars of the high prairies, camp suppers with
their exquisite frying odors. Then was the best
chance for a twelve-year-old to sneak a stiff
hooker out of the jug of some emigrant family
gone down to the creek after water, and feel
herself for a few moments as valiant and be-

dazzling as Charlotte raiding a trading post.

Yes, there were the trading post nights, too, sometimes two or three of them in a row when the train stopped for extra supplies and blacksmithing. Men fighting drunk, happy drunk and obliviously drunk on the stinging frontier firewater; Charlotte carousing in that high-toned, go-to-hell way of hers with her bachelor fellow travelers, knots of profane soldiers, buckskinned plains-wanderers, perhaps with a boozy, bewhiskered miner or two returning from the west and bent, to the company's boisterous amusement, on being publicly amorous. Strange oaths and obscenities a curious child could pick up, richer than Missouri's and with a tang of piquant newness. Sometimes there would be gorgeously heartless laughter around the whiskey barrels next morning because the town had had "a man for breakfast."

The wild country claimed her, then. It gave her a beautiful, a flamboyant vocation, sensually rich and ecstatic. Other little girls approaching their teens with her were being claimed by the stage, the enchantment of social climbing, the yen to holiness, the glamor of smart talk and intellectual distinction. But for Martha Jane always the high prairie would be the place where life had most thrilled her and she had been happiest. Always she would come back to it, comfortable, jovial, uncomplaining, bawdily at ease in her blowsy element, while other women of her sort whimpered for the sour luxuries of the raw towns.

And finally, Virginia City! Miles of low mountains flung twenty thousand miners and their hangers-on down into the boisterous, frowzy gregariousness of half a dozen miles of narrow meadow flats. Rainy days the smoke of its fires hung over it like a leaden river drowning incredible debaucheries. In fair weather tawny dust-whorls swept up from its stir into the slant planes of sunlight hundreds of feet above,—pleasantly convulsive blasts out of Bedlam.

Then torches flared, lanterns swung drunkenly, saloon fronts blazed, dance house and gambling hall entrances sparkled, camp fires flickered, guns spat forth their sudden quick jets of radiant fury. By night, after the lightless prairies, the flats were a torrent of lurid ecstasies. For a child, utterly uncontrolled, half houseless, free to go and come as she pleased, with perfect endurance and bodily activity, with endless curiosities, here were all the excitements of a world to discover.

Huge miners swaggered by, tighter than the malarious young sports of Princeton had ever dreamed of being, and yet carrying it. Silent and glassy-eyed, they would bet over the card-tables and the wheels of fortune piles of gold-dust that would have bought up all the farms that all the Canary ancestors had owned since the Revolution. Their alcoholic and amazingly obscene glees roared out of gaudy drinking palaces and up the paths to their hill-perched cabins. Choruses of male demons yelled all night over prize fights that went a hundred and forty-five rounds. Tumbling and wrestling they would clutter the mucky streets with exhausted stupefaction, with sheer abandon of animal spirits, or halt the exuberant traffic with silent, hard-breathing disputes where knives were drawn to settle a Civil War argument or title to a prostitute. Their jargon was everywhere racier, more articulate, more charmingly verbose than the bull-whackers' and the plainsmen's; their profanity booming over it richer in proportion to their congregated inventive genius.

Gamblers howled the strange terms of their

specialties over the heads of the tightly-wedged
crowds in vast new rooms radiant with mirrors,
chandeliers, polished glasses, silver, gleaming
liquors,—all the imaginable splendors. From
windows and doorways, dully rich with subdued crimson lights, women leered with amor-
ousness, called to all men with pert, shrill de-
mandings or in the whining tones of simulated
longing. Dance houses screeched all night
with the tireless fiddles, shook to the pound of
drums and hard-beaten pianos, the shuffle of
rough-shod feet and the sway of ungainly
bodies seeking ecstasy in the ponderous mood of
giants. Their walls and windows exhaled an
exciting air of the tension of long-thwarted
appetites, were shivered now and then with un-
earthly yells of Freudian delight. One or two
still bigger buildings, the burlesque theaters,
with their narrow grimy stages, dark, pocket-
like booths for boxes and cleared floor for
drinking and dancing between the acts, rocked
to huge gusts of laughter which a half-grown
girl well schooled in backwoods humor could
recognize as pornographic.

Smells assaulted her everywhere along with
the endless change of sights and sounds: smells
of the gulch creek damps, of rotting logs, fresh-

From "Beyond the Mississippi, 1833-'67," by Albert D. Richardson..

THE HURDY-GURDY HOUSE, VIRGINIA, MONTANA

In Calamity Jane's Youth a Hurdy-Gurdy Did Not Mean a Barrel Organ

sawn timbers, upturned earth; of slaughter
houses heaving off beef and pork hunks for
these ravenous appetites, too busy to clean up;
smells of incredibly compounded liquors; of
the sweat on unwashed laborious bodies; of
punk sticks; opium pipes and sour wash in the
Chinese settlements; of the hearty perfumes
of painted women pretending to luxury as well
as pleasure. Miles of rank, noisy, incessantly
vivid life swarming huddled between black
mountain masses in the intimate intoxicating
dark.

All that first autumn Martha Jane, utterly
free to her own devices, ran like a sprite with
the stream of depravity and absorbed it. The
secrets, the argot, the billingsgate of the broth-
els and dance houses she picked up as little
girls back east learned their company manners
and their school games; and doubtless, by comparison, found that the gambols of the hill
billies in Missouri had been tiresomely innocent, rustic festivals. Gamblers' tricks and
gamblers' wealth, the miners' Brobdingnagian
lewdness became her admiration as other girls
of her generation esteemed men for their impeccable proprieties, their perfect Victorian
dignity. Hanging about saloon doors, crowd-

ing within the entrance when the milling of
patrons was too confused for her to be noticed,
the more gorgeous sports and drink-buyers, the
more successful bar-room pugilists became her
idols as later little girls, just reaching the secret
adoration stage, were to be smitten with
matinée stars and Yale football heroes.

She knew hunger and cold, perhaps for the
first time in her life. Bob was right about the
worthlessness of his mining talents, Charlotte
equally wrong in her hopes for him as a gambler. Professionals and amateurs alike took
money from this "tin horn" of shoddy trickeries. Charlotte went her own gait at last with
no hindrance from his vanquished sense of the
proprieties. But trail hardships had done for
the remains of her Princeton effulgence. The
dance houses had no fortunes for a fading,
harsh-tempered sot of middle age, in competi-
tion with the buxom girls with friends from
all the diggings of Nevada and California, who
kept their heads and their looks through the
interminable debauches of their patrons by
winking the bar-tenders to fill their glasses with
cold tea.

So for the last week of 1864 the Canary
parents failed to come home, whatever that

meant. They forgot, were too drunk, too busy. What was the difference? Next to the last night of the year in Montana cold Martha Jane and her two little sisters stood on a Virginia City street corner in their calico shifts and begged something, a meal, the price of a warm bed, a piece of candy, perhaps a nip out of a New Year's bottle. Their first victim proved to be a moral merchant, one of the town's few supporting church members. They may have been looking for a tipsy miner to give away gold dust, and picking up the solid citizen may have been a mistake. They were not, even at that age, the kind of little girls to go about asking things of the sort of people who called their gifts charity.

But what were the odds? The solid citizen and his wife,—the name was Fergus and they called in some neighbors named Castner,— proved quite as satisfactory as boozily sentimental miners would have been, and no doubt considerably more practical. The Castners and the Ferguses had three probably dirty little girls in their guest beds that night, fed them enormously and sent them away with cast-off clothing enough to face a Montana winter on its own ground. True, they rushed immedi-

ately to the reporter of the *Montana Post* with
the incident.   It appeared in the paper, no
doubt veraciously, that Bob was a no-account
gambler and Charlotte was the "lowest grade"
of mining camp outcast and that something
ought to be done about it.

What of it?   Charlotte and Bob might be
fit objects for the attentions of a non-existent
Children's Aid Society and as thoroughly demoralized as their country-bred incompetence
for wild life on a truly berserk scale could
make them.   But Virginia City was still a place
where you could always eat if you were willing
to wait a little while and do it at strange hours;
where you could always get clothes enough to
warm your back if your tough, country-bred
little body could stand a few hours' siege of the
cold.   For a child of a Missouri farm slum, this
beautifully lurid town, which you could trust,
in depravity or respectability, to feed and clothe
you, was still the nearest credible approach to
heaven.   A place where, when you were a big,
dashing, beautiful woman as Charlotte had
been five years ago, you could go to hell amid a
crescendo of unfailing excitements, with a loud
noise.

It was, also, she would have known if she

had understood the long words in favor with traveling elocutionists and jury orators, the place where she was taken in charge by destiny. Missouri had predisposed her and the wanderings with the bull trains had seasoned her; but Virginia City fated her to become Calamity Jane.

I wish it were possible to follow the next steps in her progress with more assurance. Her story is that the family clung to Alder Gulch through 1865 and part of 1866 until her father died. This seems probable enough. Bob had evidently suffered enough disillusionments to crowd him feebly out of the picture. With or without him, the Canarys were hardly in the way of making money enough to leave.

Next, by this account, Charlotte and Martha Jane went up a neighboring gulch into the mining town of Blackfoot. There, after a year of laundering clothes for miners, Charlotte died, presumably of some virtuous pioneer malady like wash-tub pneumonia.

This, however, has indications of being a pious legend invented in later years to impress strangers, curious about her celebrity, with her impeccable parentage. Charlotte, quite pos-

sibly, took in washing at odd times when
charms had no market and her efficiency promised to pay a little.   Therefore, she was a poor
but lady-like camp laundress.   To give the tale
color there is added the sottish old woman in
whose care Jane was supposed to have been left
after Charlotte's virtuous passing, and from
whom she got her schooling in low life.   This,
certainly, is the typical alibi used by ninety-nine
wandering Cyprians out of a hundred, to account for the miscarriage of an uplifting and
refined early training through the hazards of
moral fortune.

But there is another story, also apparently on
Jane's spoken authority, which she seems to
have told when she wished to impress other
audiences with her precocity rather than her
innocence.   By this, the Widow Canary went
to Blackfoot with a small stake for a profitable
investment, acquired a substantial establishment, became Madame Canary and called the
most enticing bagnio in town by the subtle
name of "The Bird-Cage."

Blackfoot is a ghost town now, or rather but
the fading memory of the ghost town.   Even
its records, such as they were, were destroyed
by the fire of '69, and no "Bird Cage" was

among the casualties, nor among its colorful and reasonably complete police reports in the *Montana Post* for several years previous. There may have been such an institution, for the Charlotte of Princeton days, if reasonably sober, would have been capable of calling forth executive talents when charm was no longer enough to support her in a style to which she would like to become accustomed. But the probabilities are against it. Charlotte in her Montana phase had got over the habit of being reasonably sober. She may have talked hopefully, when moderately drunk, of founding a "Bird-Cage." But I doubt if she ever interested the necessary capital.

By the laundress' story Charlotte died in 1867. And by the Bird-Cage story she acquired a second husband, as not infrequently happened in the west with successful Bird-Cage proprietresses, and moved to Salt Lake City in 1867, to vanish later amid the dizzy goings and comings of her more celebrated daughter. Which is one to believe? All we know certainly is that sometime before the end of 1866 four young boys travelling up from Utah found her in Bannock learning the rudiments of western underworld etiquette from the famous woman gambler, Madame Moustache. They sold her eggs and their boy and girl acquaintance was both slight and innocent enough. But one of them remembers her after sixty years as showing far more sophistication with life in rowdy places than was encouraged among the Mormon virgins.

Jane was fifteen in 1867, a strapping, cheerful, rough-mannered, generous wench, with her mother's coppery-red hair, challenging brown eyes and easily postured figure. She had her mother's profane contempt for the proprieties sharpened by an appetite for bawdy pleasures and a humorous tolerance for the ways of the mining camp underworld. Her mother's earlier instinct for deeds of erratic generosity was strong in her, stimulated a little by her father's gentleness. Whether she lay in a hasty Blackfoot burial ground or retired into the respectabilities of the lower Gentile society of Salt Lake City, Charlotte had given Martha Jane as much as she had to give.

Both accounts, after all, agree that Jane was in Salt Lake City by the end of 1867. Perhaps, instead of Charlotte, it was the sottish foster-mother who had won a husband named Hart, and Jane came posing as her daughter.

The metropolis of 500,000 square miles of mining, bull-whacking and Indian-fighting territory could hardly, whatever her chaper-onage, have held her without furthering her education in lewdness. Soldiers and the celeb-rities of the freight and express routes con-gregated here with gold-panners, successful and desperately otherwise; with gamblers, pimps, and curious tourists. It was, by all accounts, a welter of lively debauchery which yokels from the gulches and Missouri farm-steads must have found positively metropolitan in its elegance. The Mormons encouraged it in the triple conviction that it would bring the wrath of the Lord down on the Gentiles, that it helped to reassure the saved saints of their superior piety and that it was good business. The approaching railroads, building across the plains and through the Sierras toward Nevada, were already feeding the town's night life with job-seekers, discharged laborers, spree-hungry laborers with their savings, dissolute construc-tion bosses off for holidays, and equally disso-lute capitalists with time and money on their hands waiting for investments to turn up. It was Virginia City over again, multiplied by ten and with the charm of luxury and the solidity of permanence added.

Martha Jane faced it for a winter, but one suspects that it abashed her. Her taste had been formed for the brawling life of towns where vice was uncorrupted with magnificence. In the spring she was off for wanderings that from now on were to be habitual.

She was with the soldiers at Fort Steele and Fort Bridger. She was with the railway construction gangs at Piedmont, in Wyoming. It was the propitious time for a girl of her outlook and experiences to be "ruined." Perhaps it had happened before. This, at any rate, was the year to fix it in the Calamity Jane legends. And of course it could not, after she had become a celebrity, be a mere private soldier or a nameless miner, hovering about Charlotte Canary-Hart or the sottish foster-mother until the prize fell to him. It must be an officer, and he must have a name. So the legend called him Lieut. Somers and—rather mawkishly— added that Jane bore him a son whose adoption she carefully secured from an upright family.

It is simply to be remembered that when she was of an age to challenge the proprieties of life, rankly and boisterously for the sake of her flamboyant pleasure, she challenged them. She made her play against respectability as early as possible, and she stuck to it.

It was about this time, I believe, that she abandoned women's society almost altogether. It was the instinctive thing to do and so, for her, the easiest.

She had preferred little boys for playmates even in the Princeton days. They could throw corncobs at you hard and straight enough to make it really interesting. They would go tearing through the woods with you, swim with you, wrestle with you, do a hundred things that other little girls, with their dainty better-than-you-are airs would avoid because they might tear their pinafores, dirty their faces, wet their feet, or merely because it wasn't "lady-like." Now the grown men out west were the Missouri boys all over again, but infinitely more glamorous. The things you could do with them were not merely mischievous, they were deliciously dangerous: The long rides over the plains or into the mountains with real varmints to shoot at instead of squirrels, and with Indians possibly to pot-shot at you; the wild grip they would seize you with in the dances until you shuddered with delight; the almost incredible hilarity of their carousals and the equally magnificent fury of their rages, when a chance misunderstanding, or better, a rivalry for your own momentary favor, raised a fight.

Martha Jane desired them now with the strength of her healthy, perfectly exercised body. She would fix on one particularly gorgeous frontiersman and desire his nearness and his embraces unstintedly for a whole week. Or she would encourage a dozen charming rawhiders of chance acquaintance and, with a loud guffaw at her possessiveness, desire them all equally and simultaneously. Not that her possessing, or not possessing, really mattered. There was opportunity enough and time enough for that, the way they were running after her and with so many years of youth stretching ahead. If they wanted her badly enough, pressed her energetically, perhaps they could take her. If not, to show how much she cared, they could go out, she would profligately tell them, and get scalped by a Sioux squaw.

But however they approached her, it was good to have them around. Simply the distillation of their thronging maleness gave her exaltation, made her feel more than she was. She could ride more daringly with them, shoot better, curse more splendidly, drink deeper and more triumphantly, find a better relish in the jests of their underworld. With them she was, according to her lights, more witty and more seductive than herself. Not for her was this sitting in tawdry rooms and blaring dance houses waiting for them. She must have men with her, with her always, with her in droves.

This was easy, because there were so many of them,—five, ten, fifty, a hundred to a woman in each settlement. They were so excited to have you about, so overwhelmingly concerned with the sight and shape of you, that it was almost like being made love to even when you did not especially hit it off personally with some new group of strangers. So she could always, if she made a point of it, go where they were going, do as much as she liked of what they were doing, and be touched or not as she pleased. If it was an embarrassing, not a permissible, expedition for women, they would smuggle her in and take her along somehow.

No one, certainly, could have had less traditionally feminine inhibitions about going. The wildness, the discomfort of the open country, merely delighted her hardiness. The dance-house girls, the forehanded vampires of the gulch and construction camp tenderloins could have all the delusions they pleased about keeping their dignity and increasing their incomes by making the men come to them. To hell with that! If Martha Jane wanted men, the whole world could know it and go break its neck. Charlotte's love of shocking anemic women who didn't want men and prissy, posturing little wenches who pretended they didn't, came back upon her with a savage flamboyance. Martha Jane would show 'em whose business it was.

So she started off on the trails hunting for the places where men were thickest. There was no use going back to the Virginia City neighborhood. The gulch was dying already from overworked deposits, orderly as a church now with its tightly organized courts and police force. The miners who stayed there to work for the big producing corporations on wages had brought wives out from the east or had married dance-house girls, and were living as respectably as parsons. A girl aspiring to limitless male companionship would be out of luck there, like Charlotte back in Princeton. The current points of allurement were the railroad construction towns,—Piedmont, South Pass City, Rawlins, Green River.

True, the boundless frenzies of gulch night life may have been lacking. No construction gang ever drew such a bonus for track-laying speed that they could rival a lucky prospector's syndicate out to spend $50,000 in a night and doing it. Still, all through 1868 and down to '69 the railway towns were good enough. Pay-nights the funds in circulation were as vast as in the mining camps. And what was superior to the miners' spending possibilities, for an hour or two at least, until the gamblers began to take their toll, everybody had some of it.

Champagne corks popped among the section bosses, barrels of whiskey floated the spirits of the laborers higher than the howls of the timber wolves in the neighboring forests. Lurching between the roaring shacks they showed off their tricks of Bowery thuggery, Civil War close-in fighting, western—and highly per-sonal—marksmanship; their excitingly various ways of love-making, violent, ostentatious, half-burlesqued, dangerous. Timber-cutters, hairy, half-savage giants from Michigan and Wisconsin, with songs and legends that were almost a folk lore, charged down from their mountain camps and raided the effete shovel-heavers like Apaches.   The shovel-heavers raided back and returned with blood on the ends of their picks.   Martha Jane ran with one side and then with the other, according as her latest infatuation moved her.   Whichever side it was, she cursed with an eloquence which the critical creative artists of either camp were glad to acknowledge as picturesque.   She learned to land a buffet from her fists, when the emergency demanded, with a force in the blow that was not much inferior to a practiced pick-wielder's; to pack a gun in the most convenient recess of her outer garments and "throw down" with it—always harmlessly, it seems—when gang fights threatened her lover of the moment or her charms were in danger of being tasted by unwelcome suitors.

But it was not all night life.   She could camp out near Laramie, according to the liveliest recollection, with her favorite lumber-jack for weeks at a time and ride out over the mountains as with the hunters on the Overland trek.   Far ahead of the towns where the track construction ended were the camps of the shovel experts making the grades and the embankment for the ties to lie on.   She could pack herself in a friendly bull train supplying them and ride back and forth for days. If a Puritanical wagon boss was sniffy about the outfit's morals, she could borrow a teamster's clothes and wear them. This made it easy, with her harsh, somewhat masculine features, to escape detection. On the way, when a teamster wanted to malinger, she could take his bull-whip over the easy places and tramp along showing the skill with the cracker she had learned on the overland trip. When she got to the grading camp, the open secret of her coming would be passed around, and almost certainly some oaf of the section gang would be on hand ready to entrust pick and shovel to her husky shoulders while he slept off in the shade or the warmth of the bunk house the effects of last night's whiskey.

In that country of rumors and the itch for marvels, she was growing a reputation by these unfeminine dalliances. The men who saw her perform them knew that they were unadulterated hokum. A good-natured camp trollop cruising with the timber bands, handling a pick, hoisting ties on her shoulder, cracking the bull whip,—it was an amusing trick to put over on the boss while his back was turned; a grotesque parody on men's serious work no less delightful because of the slight aroma of lewd interest in Jane's being on such expeditions at all.

But these were not the tales they told when they got back to the towns. Had you heard that that Canary girl,—yes, the same one that walked away with a quart of whiskey the other night cursing like your grandfather when the bee stung him,—had put on men's clothes and was chopping ties up in the mountains? Or took a bull-whacker's place on the last trip to the grading camps when a regular teamster was down sick? Or helped put down a whole section of ties the other morning just to let one of the boys play out his all-night game of seven-up?

By the time the talk reached the next town it was more startling still. There was a woman fifty miles up the line in men's clothes and two guns on her hip, doing a regular section-hand's job. Jane something or other was her name. Jane what?

She was less than seventeen and she was acquiring celebrity. What she did was of no consequence, impromptu, inefficient probably, a few moments' ostentation—like Charlotte's Princeton errands—all for the sake of the joke. All the same, no other woman of the camp demi-monde was doing it. They were sitting in their frowzily scented little bedroom parlors and waiting for the men to come and love them, in a jag and for a price. Jane was out with the men roughing it, playing at being as good a man as they were, being the camp's ideal of a dead game sport. So long as they fed her and gave her their cast-off clothing to wear, she didn't care whether she made anything off them or not. A good-hearted hussy, hard as nails, but one of their own kind. There was a justifiable fame in being that even if they could have chopped the ties and laid the rails and built the grades without her.

Then in 1869 a President rode out in sublimely Pullmanized state to drive a golden spike at Promontory Point, and the railroad was finished. The construction towns faded into tank towns and track-walkers' stations or débris-caches on the desert. Their barbaric splendors were mourned. Their inhabitants scattered over the west to squat on mining claims or ranch land. They returned to "the States" to lie about Indians and their good conduct, or, easing themselves into routine jobs on the new "system," settled down to being nagged by hastily summoned mates from the east who disapproved of the local climate, manners and groceries. The railroad had ceased to be a male world in effervescence. Where to go next?

According to her story, Jane drifted that winter to Cheyenne. The plausibilities uphold her. There was a lull in gold-strike activities except in Nevada, and she would hardly have gone there among the Chinks whom the Central Pacific had used to push its tracks into Ogden and who at that time, she had surely been led to believe by their Union Pacific rivals, were the representative citizenry of the country beyond the Mormon settlements. On the other hand, her own friends of the construction camps were gravitating to Cheyenne, lured almost as much by the prospect of jobs in the new division carshops as by its safety from Indians and its superior saloon life. The town had already a resident population of nearly 3,000, a figure which the constant inflow of transients frequently doubled. Cow country, Indian army, railroaders and miners were to meet there during the next dozen years more numerously than at any other point east of the mountains, making its tenderloin as uproarious as Virginia

City's, but more various and spacious. In the winter of 1869-70, in any event, it was the most male spot on her immediate horizon. If she had not gone, she would have belied her nature.

Even Cheyenne could hardly teach her anything new in the way of rowdiness. But she could use the town to acquire a few hundred more acquaintances and to presume more and more startlingly on the privileges of her growing celebrity. Here for the first time apparently she swaggered in men's clothes up and down the streets of a town which made some pretense of respecting the proprieties. Here she first firmly established her right to drink at bars hitherto reserved exclusively for males.

Was she not by accepted legend the only girl who had worked for the Union Pacific? And did not that entitle her to scorn the decorum which relegated "demi-monde ladies" to dance house bars and the family entrances only, and put "real ladies" completely out of the picture?

About this time, or possibly a year or two later, since such matters can be dated only by the most shadowy recollections, a new bartender in the town, with the restraints of Denver's drinking proprieties firmly engrained in his nature, declined to give her service. He found himself looking into the barrel of her pistol and heard a hearty contralto 'voice commanding, "I reckon you don't know who I am. Say, young feller, don't you know if Calamity Jane wasn't a lady, you might be setting up drinks right now for this blanky-blank crowd?" A bystander interposed at this point with a sufficient explanation. Also, as was often characteristic of her patronage, he paid for her drink.

But a minor celebrity has certain disturbing disadvantages. When one's notoriety is connected wholly with transactions, like railroad building, now dead and done with, it tends to die out and its privileges to pass with it. Yet Martha Jane's brief experience had whetted her appetite for bigger and more privileged ostentations rather than less. Solely on this account, I am convinced, the legend dawned shortly after the Cheyenne winter that she had enlisted with General Custer as a scout.

This claim is the prime basis of her fame as an outstanding historical pioneer character, as the heroine of half a dozen wild western dime novels and of various sentimental romances of slightly higher respectability. Yet it seems wholly preposterous.

Such a personage as a Mollie Pitcher of the

plains cavalry could not have thrived without enjoying a tangible notoriety in every branch of the plains army and wherever civilians saw its forces in campaign. The mere rarity of women in the west in Indian-fighting days would have exalted the most modest actual performance on her part into a regional saga. Yet no government record or army tradition vouches for her, and all old soldiers of the Indian wars I have been able to find deny the lore of her scouting with more or less profane amusement.

The nearer one comes to the actual scene of Jane's heroic performances, the more they vanish. They were good stories to tell a hundred miles away, and better still at five hundred when no embarrassing witnesses were present. They were good to spread that celebrity around which had proved so agreeable in the Cheyenne winter after the railroad-building days. They were good to win drinks with and to secure those rare and inestimable and so pleasantly ostentatious bar-room privileges. They made it possible for her to be more with men and with more men at a time than she could have been otherwise. They set her apart, as Charlotte would have enjoyed being set apart, from the anemic and felinely organized women whom both mother and daughter scorned and loved to outshine in superior gaudiness. It was worth making up any kind of improbable lie about yourself to outshine them as your superior vitality entitled you; all the sweeter when you put this rout of whining, fat-witted gold-diggers in their place, not by merit but by a hoax.

All the same it is reasonably possible that Martha Jane did go out with a military expedition in the spring of 1870,—the first of many. She had discovered the charms of soldiers before; witness her visits to Fort Bridger and Fort Steele. She would certainly have enormously enlarged her military acquaintance during the Cheyenne winter. Her new friends formed the biggest body of men to go off womanless into the prairie country where she could show off her hardihood and be at the same time the center of a situation most to her taste. There would be small doubt of her risking such an escapade if she thought she could get away with it.

And her chances were good. Riding along as a woman cavalryman was of course out of the question. Companies were checked up too often, the inspections by authority were too rigid. But the Indian army was supplied by bull trains, operating as civilian outfits under contract, where the discipline was much less strict. Martha Jane by 1870 was almost as useful on a bull train as a man and knew by the best accounts virtually every moderately or grossly dissolute bull-whacker around Cheyenne intimately. With such an outfit and a hundred or more good friends to keep her secret, she could stow away without risk of detection almost indefinitely. If not of the cavalry precisely, she would at least follow along with its rear guard most of the time and be decidedly in the presence of the whole army when it paused for long term encampments.

Her story is that she was trekked with the army down to a campaign against the Arizona Apaches in 1870-71. This is not a complete impossibility, since officers were not so much on the watch for a familiar camp-follower as they were to be a few years later and Jane herself may have been more discreet. But what is reported of her other movements makes it doubtful. The old-timers began to see her on trails that were, whatever their pleasing turbulence, a long way from the Apache country.

One fairly coherent recollection places her

in a cattle driving train for the famous Majors Russell and Waddell between Kansas City and Denver. Thus quite possibly, she went no more than a hundred and twenty miles from Cheyenne to Denver with a military detachment and then deserted for an outfit which promised more excitement than the somewhat rigidly policed desert camps of the soldiers. It would have been like her to sponsor a yarn of scouting in Arizona on just that.

Some time, too, within the next few months, she appeared in the Kansas cow towns,—Abilene, Hayes City. For the time being, there she seems to have suffered a relapse into femininity. One Pat Tucker of Livingston, Mont., remembers her at Hayes City, where her beauty and gentle bearing, together with a certain elegance of costume, got her among the chivalrously admiring cow-hands coming with droves up from Texas the name of the "Prairie Queen."

She seems, too, to have imposed on the public a yarn even more improbable than that of her Apache scoutings. A freighter and lucky gambler of the name of Allegheny Dick was with her, and to make things right with the rising Kansas conventions, or possibly to bring back

From *"Beyond the Mississippi, 1853-'67,"* by *Albert D. Richardson.*

BUILDING THE UNION PACIFIC RAILROAD IN NEBRASKA

The Arrival of a Young Female Co-laborer Was Naturally Hailed with Something More Than Idle Curiosity

an amusing tale to the Cheyenne dance houses, she represented herself as his innocent daughter. The name of Canary seems not to have been mentioned in this idyll, Allegheny Dick not answering to any definite patronymic.

Shortly, in any case, he left her an "orphan." He went west, and, as the phrase went, "turned up missing," which was as pleasant an evasion for being unlucky at gambling or tired of a mistress as for running afoul of Indians. Then the pose of refinement seems to have slackened, if not that of innocence. In Dodge City about 1872, in the presence of reputable and sober witnesses, a cowboy ballad singer, with the insinuating name of Darling Bob Mackay, presumed on his talents for the risqué and asked her an intimate question concerning her lower lingerie. She filled the air with shrill and slightly obscene rebukes for his bawdiness, and his sombrero with warning bullets.

That year again Wyoming seems to have claimed her. Quite possibly it was by a cattle trail up which her new Texan friends were driving their "doagies" to the northern pasturage. Having proved it to bull-whackers, section hands and soldiers, it would be like her to show cowboys now that she was of a huskier breed than the perfume-lapped dance-house hussies.

But her own desire was to represent her adventures in this period as strictly military. She was at Fort Saunders, Wyoming, her autobiography insists, the winter and spring of 1872. She was off with the cavalry again in the summer for a little running skirmish with the Indians called the Muscle Shells War. There may be a wraith of truth in it. Male companionship was even thicker at the military posts in winter than in the cow towns. She would have sought them out if there were enough males going along that way to make her journey interesting. She would have ridden a few hundred miles toward the Muscle Shells War with the first handy supply train. That would still leave plenty of time for a late summer and autumn expedition into Kansas and the crushing of Darling Bob's familiarities. A strong and attractive wench, enamored of trail life, could have traveled about with the soldiers, in fact, and still found opportunity for two or three trips a year back and forth between Kansas and Wyoming.

But however she distributed her activities geographically, one finds her crowning legend of 1872 entirely unplausible. The cavalry by this lurid piece of "autobiography" were attacking a Nez Perce village. Jane in her scout's trappings joined in the charge with Captain "Pat" Egan's company. The charge had wheeled back, with the captain, as became a military leader posing for the steel engraving artists, turning last.

At this crucial moment, his horse fell dead with a dozen bullet wounds and the captain lay pinned under its flank with a hundred warpainted braves rushing forward to make him prisoner. Jane whirled her horse, beat them to him, helped the captain free himself and mount behind her. Together they galloped away in a haze of Nez Perce missiles with the captain orating gratefully: "Jane, you're a wonderful little woman to have around in times of calamity. From now on your name's Calamity Jane."

Unfortunately, this epic has fatal discrepancies. Not a single old soldier that I have been able to find who served in the Indian armies with Egan ever heard of it until years afterward. The captain himself, a fighting Celt who pronounced his name with the accent on the last syllable and was given to indulging all emotions explosively, including gratitude, is never quoted as referring to it in all the scores of pages which eye witness chroniclers of the Indian campaigns devoted to his colorful personality. There is no record of a charge attack by his troop on an Indian village in 1872. When Captain Egan did charge a Sioux camp in the dead of winter several years later, two authors of Indian war books riding with him, one of them bridle to bridle, did not observe that he was even for an instant put out of the combat or required a rescuer.

In fact, the only traceable relation between Calamity and the captain occurred nearly four years later when Jane and a rare girl friend after her own heart borrowed cavalry uniforms for a few weeks at Fort Laramie and went about enjoying the novelties of barrack life and performing the necessary military courtesies. But the explosive Captain "Pat" was so far from feeling gratitude that he was overwhelmed with a profane chagrin to discover that he had spent a week returning the scandalous salutes of "a couple of God-damned chippies." He enthusiastically issued orders to have his "rescuer" chased off the reservation and not a single growl was heard in the barracks, by the best surviving recollections, that he owed her better treatment. The simple fact begins to appear that Jane, despite her talents and her amiabilities, was more the celebrity than the historian.

Yet in these years she acquired her name somehow. There are almost as many explanations as there are old-timers. Calamity was associated with her because she carried guns ostentatiously and was given to inviting it; because she suffered several successive buggy-smashing accidents in Cheyenne and was considered unlucky; because she bashed the heads of various insufficiently ardent lovers and a peace officer or two and therefore might be considered to bring it with her; because of her bedraggled and notoriously down-at-the-heels appearance when returning from her trail expeditions or in liquor; because in the cow towns she had found the charming epithet on an inconspicuous dance-house girl, otherwise named Grace or Polly or Annie, and had basely appropriated it; because her lovers, sometimes miscalled husbands, developed habits of dying violently.

At any rate, she seems to have secured public consent to her acquisition by the time she discouraged Darling Bob's pornographic allusions in Dodge City, within a year after she had been merely Allegheny Dick's charming daughter and the prairie queen. Self-invented or however bestowed, she was shrewd enough to grasp the name's merit. Pickhandle Nan, Madame Moustache, Kitty the Schemer, Rowdy Kate,—in an era of grotesque nomenclature these were amusing enough. But Calamity Jane had a macabre splendor all its own and beyond them, undertones of violence and defiance, of gunplay and delirium tremens, of prairie thunder, mountain whiskey, hell, high water and sudden death, that the best of the others lacked.

She rolled it on her tongue, she screeched it, tumbled it out with a mouthful of oaths in melodramatic contralto, and obviously loved it. "I'm Calamity Jane and this drink's on the house," she howled at hesitating Wyoming bartenders. "I'm Calamity Jane. Get to hell out of here and let me alone," were her first proud words when awakened from a somewhat unlady-like stupor in a Cheyenne woodshed. "I'm Calamity Jane and I sleep when and where I damn please," she informed a con-

ventional young man from the east who returned to his quarters in an impeccable Cheyenne rooming house one Sunday afternoon in
1873 to find her stretched out in full bull-
whacker's toggery on his otherwise inviolate
couch. "Calam's here," the crowd roared in
the Cheyenne dance house and the intermis-
sion gayeties of McDaniel's Theater. "You
bet Calam's here," would come back the
squaw-like war-whoop coupled with invoca-
tions to the sons of all the indignities. "Now
let her rip."

Such a name itself conferred privileges, lus-
tre. Celebrity, flamboyance, notoriety would
grow up around it even if she did not trouble
to invent legends herself. If one was to pose
as the feminine divinity of western wildness,
there was nothing like beginning as a walking
slogan.

Even so, she had her mild phases. Being
temporarily out of feminine apparel she borrowed a dress from a Cheyenne woman to get
a job as waitress. She never brought the dress
back, but served the traveling public modestly
for nearly a month. In 1874 she became so
enamored of respectability that she "married"
a brakeman in Rawlins and kept house for

him neatly and conventionally as long as his charm lasted. For months, too, in the early '70s she worked at various respectable feminine employments at Green River and South Pass City. A family named Robinson thought her an extraordinarily nice girl to have grown up on the plains and in the mining camps, more agreeable and witty than most, more intelligent, kinder-hearted.

A little girl in the family fell sick in an epidemic of what frontier medicine called "the black diphtheria." Jane ignored the dangers of contagion and nursed her until she died. For thirty years after, there was at least one home to which Calam could retreat for her occasional, and gradually less frequent, splurges in respectability; where her pride in her reputation as a hard character was taken for no more than a conscientious pose.

In the spring of 1875, by the best surviving notations of fifty-two-year-old gossip, her current military infatuation was personal. He was a droll, light-drinking and exceedingly efficient infantry sergeant by the name of Frank Siechrist, and he was ordered to accompany the expedition of Lieutenant-Colonel

Dodge to the Black Hills in the Sioux reservation country as escort to a party of civilian minerologists. Custer had reconnoitered the Black Hills the previous summer and certain more or less uninvited camp followers, bringing their pans and pebble-washing equipment along, were touting up a gold discovery. The government wished to know the worth of the find and then get the struggle over with the Sioux as soon as possible.

Calamity smuggled herself along with the bull train and had, by authentic reports of surviving veterans, the most successful military expedition on her record. She did not scout and she rescued no captains, but she did something, which from her viewpoint of the military arts and sciences required even more adroitness. She circulated with her usual sociability among the soldiers and the bull-whackers and enjoyed the stimulating companionship of Mr. Siechrist in the long summer twilights, but she kept her presence from the official knowledge of Lieutenant-Colonel Dodge. It is the only expedition which, according to reasonably positive testimony, she stayed with from beginning to end.

She came out with intimations of a new

object in life. Mr. Siechrist remained charming and so did some others, but here in the Black Hills was the making of gold camp life as ecstatic and super-abundantly masculine as Virginia City's in its heyday. The region was not, to be sure, worth an ambitious young woman's exclusive attentions in the summer of 1875. There were, after all, hardly more than six hundred miners in it. These were scattered in bands too small to be interesting, hiding out in the gulches from the cavalry which was diligently employed in deporting them to protect the Sioux in their reservation rights, and from the Sioux who were doing still more drastic protective work on their own account. The miners were thus temporarily inhibited from a male community life on a scale which Jane was educated to appreciate. But there was no doubt about the gold being there—even the minerologists admitted it—and Jane saw signs, once the country was opened to settlement, of the most exhilarating gold rush since the Montana days.

The next spring it happened. The government had made an effort to buy the Black Hills from the Sioux for the price of a modest New Jersey subdivision, and the warriors had coolly demanded $70,000,000. Therefore, the Sioux were declared ousted, and the miners told to go in, file claims and save their scalps when possible. Hence, the towns of Custer and Crook City had populations ranging up toward the 2,000 mark by Easter. Up in the northern fastnesses, Deadwood Gulch had forty claims staked by January and in April was forced, by the traffic problem of bull trains milling about in its narrow flats, to organize itself as a city.

It is a supreme tribute to Sergeant Siechrist's amatory allurements that Calamity was not among the first arrivals. Still, that winter and spring the possibilities of the Hills were yet somewhat chaotic, while the pleasures of army life were secure and better than ever. The posts from Kansas to Utah were full of recruits and hastily summoned units from the southwest, mobilizing for the campaign against the Sioux. The cordons which Crook, Terry, Custer and Gibbon were to lead out in the spring were the most numerous the northern Indian army had ever assembled. Men in blue were never so abundant, so generous with their time and liquor purchases, or so inspired by the prospect of serious fighting ahead to make the most of the pleasures of post life while they had them.

Calamity alternated between the gayeties of Cheyenne and the thicker atmosphere of an institution for ladies, ambiguously known in soldiers' slang as a "hog ranch," on the outskirts of the reservation at Fort Laramie. The situation was too delightfully tense and insistent, too concretely pleasant to desert for the joys of two or three ill-established and unsettled mining camps four hundred miles away. The prospectors, the gamblers, the bar-tenders and other charmingly loose camp followers were departing from Cheyenne for the Black Hills daily, but only in dribbles of a few score at a time. But it was common knowledge, and to Jane wholly seductive, that Crook would start off from Fort Laramie with not less than fifteen hundred men, including Sergeant Siechrist, and probably without a single other woman to compete against her.

She was in Cheyenne when she heard that he was to march immediately. She hired a horse and buggy at the daylight conclusion of the McDaniels Theater revels. The next afternoon, horse in a lather and axles squeaking from exhausted grease and the hard usage of a pace equivalent to a slightly under-par Ford's, she rode into Fort Laramie in time to be off with the last available bull train.

That campaign, by the autobiography's testimony, saw the summit of her military labors. She scouted for Sioux on the Rosebud. She took her place on the firing line in the skirmishes. She carried messages alone across the plains from Crook to Terry, from Crook to Custer. She would have been the only woman victim in the massacre of the Little Big Horn, if in her last effort to reach Custer's column with "important dispatches," she had not swum the Platte River in flood, taken pneumonia and been laid up during the crucial weeks in the hospital at Fort Fetterman.

Unfortunately, the only plausible point in the whole gasconade is that she was apparently retired from the expedition for a swimming escapade. Crook was a hard-boiled, bewhiskered disciplinarian on the most serious Indian campaign in the northern annals. The last thing he desired on the expedition was a woman in any capacity, dispatch-bearer or girl friend. Consequently, Jane spent her time hiding out in the wagon trains with unusual secretiveness. Only the inner circle of rakish privates and noncoms seems to have known that she was along at all. Then, on a hot day in June, possibly on Goose Creek near Sheridan, but more probably on Hat Creek, her passion for ostentation asserted itself and she accepted an invitation, no doubt enthusiastic, to join a military swimming party.

It was not by the flowing outlines of the modish ladies' bathing suits of 1876 that she was detected. An officer lounging by became dimly, and then officially, conscious that one of the forms splashing about in the water was decidedly out of line with the physical standards required by the U. S. regular army. He filed his report with due diligence. That night various alarmed privates and noncoms went on the 1876 equivalent for kitchen police and Calamity rode under guard in an ambulance back to Fort Fetterman. One of the most engaging military careers in American annals was over,—all but the talking.

There was no use trying to go back and she knew it. Fetterman, guarded by an awkward squad of rookies and invalids, was no longer alluring and Laramie was quite as bad. But the Black Hills, the plains were saying, were thronging with ten thousand miners,—or was it twenty thousand? There in those crazily cut gulches which last summer had reminded her, in spite of their emptiness, of the lurid nights in Blackfoot and Virginia City, they would be roistering again, breaking heads, shooting, cursing, swaggering, showing off, raining down fortunes in gold dust on delectably fastidious gamblers; above all wanting women, ready to buoy women up to the skies with their amative eagerness and their roaring comradeship. The most male place on earth!

She knew in an instant where her meat was. Damn fool that she was not to have known it before! Think of a woman of her age and experience wasting half her summer on a bunch of half-starved Indian fighters with their ten dollars a month, their rigid discipline and snooping officers too rough to appreciate a lady's feelings.

The road ran up from Cheyenne through Fort Laramie almost straight northeast over the high plains, thick with bull trains, mule trains, hired carriages, coaches, trampers, cavalcades. By the best of chronological evidence, she must have struck out straight across country from Fetterman, and with a fast horse at that. By the last of June a freighting outfit deposited her, with a shooting equipment, a stock of the latest army profanity and old miners' jargon, and a swagger that was due a new country on the make for savage celebrity. To further the excitement, she was that night and for several nights, as an observant eye-witness put it, "blind as a bat from looking at the bottom of a glass." She honored the conventions by shooting out numerous saloon lights.

Then Wild Bill came. She was approaching her climax.

She had almost certainly known Mr. James B. Hickock in Kansas and Cheyenne. By most competent testimony, the acquaintance was strictly casual and remained so. Mr. Hickock was the real thing in western derring-do and Calamity was merely a western spectacle. Mr. Hickock had killed no doubt upwards of a dozen men in his various duties of self-defense, gambling punctilio and peace officership, instead of the hundred or more who were sensationally attributed to him. But he had definitely and expertly killed them. Calamity, on the other hand, had talked exhaustively about being a scout and a rescuer of captains,

but actually had been an amusingly rakish
camp follower and a kind-hearted demi-mon-
daine with an exceptional passion for plains
life and male abundance. Wild Bill was the
sort of person to be grimly amused at such
antics, but to prefer for his intimacies solidity
rather than hokum.

Nevertheless, Mr. Hickock was reaching a
stage in his career where the spectacular was
useful to him. He was a triple-barrelled celebrity, the greatest in the west for a more or
less indeterminate period, and he had found
that it paid to look the part.

His long hair and stallion-tail moustaches,
adopted originally because of the total absence
of barbers, were worth a fortune to him when
he returned east, as he had during several recent winters, to enrich metropolitan melodrama with his acting talents. He had recently
married a circus proprietress and, while he
was not definitely connected with the enterprise, his wife had doubtless told him that the
fame of his picturesque appearance, even at a
distance, helped the show's publicity. In any
case, dressing the part would help his immediate business as a gambler in a region thronging, or soon certain to throng, with curious

tenderfeet anxious for no greater notoriety than that of having lost what their means could afford to Wild Bill Hickock. Mr. Hickock, in short, was reaching the stage where he was not so much an individual as an institution, almost a troupe.

As a troupe, in fact, he rode into Custer. There was not only Wild Bill himself, but four perfect simulacra walked abreast of him when traffic in the frowzy streets permitted, or formed a small but royally impressive Indian-file procession up and down the lanes and in and out of the saloons when traffic didn't. Next to the leader, on most appearances, came Colorado Charlie Utter, a gambler with a genius for personal pageantry who made up for his inferiority to Mr. Hickock in stature by wearing moustachios and mane even more luxuriant; indeed if envious gossip is to be believed, by treating his lustrously blond ringlets to frequent applications of the curling iron.

Behind Charlie followed Bloody Dick Seymour, atoning for the slight disharmony of his swarthiness in an otherwise strictly Nordic group by contributing an expression of peculiar ferocity, his sole title, so far as can be learned, to a name more terrible than an army with banners. The rear was brought up by two blond gentlemen of heroic proportions, unfortunately nameless to history, whom one hopes, not too confidently, Mr. Hickock did not borrow from Madame Lake-Hickock's circus.

All five had adorned themselves with buckskin suits of notably gorgeous contours and fringes even in an age when what the well dressed plains scout should wear was rapidly becoming a theatrical convention. Enormous cream-white Stetsons crowned their flowing locks, glowing amid the tattered and rain-streaked head-gear of the smeary prospectors like sunbursts of felt elegance. Revolver butts gleamed from their business pockets with the savage luster of perfect polishing. The very wood shone in the hafts of their bowie knives above sheathes oiled gaudily as harness in a horse show. When they rode, which was often, and when the crowd happened to be out and in a staring mood, their mounts were curried and clipped to a condition of positively scandalous dandyism; their saddles and bridles ornate with gewgaws like a Mexican general's.

It was as though the male chorus were assembling for a modern Robin Hood.

But these artists were enamored of perfection and open to constructive suggestions. Their show was stupendous, but they would make it bigger and better as they saw their way. Suddenly it burst upon them. Perhaps Wild Bill had the vision, but I am inclined in favor of Colorado Charlie whose talents for stage-managing western fashion shows were more consciously developed and specialized. In any case, when Calamity Jane came tumbling down upon them in an explosion of greetings in their first bar-room encounter, one of them or all of them realized in a sudden flash of genius that the troupe needed a woman.

One lady Wild Bill understudy, plus the four gentlemen and the real thing, would round it out complete. They were going to Deadwood. These Custer diggings were only color in the pans and were already wearing out. The town had already half depopulated itself to feed the milling city in the dark gulch fifty miles to the north over mountain trails. There the gold was by repute inexhaustible. There were already, by somewhat exaggerated report, five thousand miners. With a woman in their train, they could make into this metropolis of riches, violence, malign delights and macabre atmosphere an entry that would knock their eyes out. Calamity could ride like a road agent, wear men's clothes without mincing, flourish two guns like a desperado, drink at any bar in the west without question or feminine mannerisms, and was already more of a celebrity in her own right than Colorado Charlie, Bloody Dick and two unknowns combined. She got the job.

They gave her two nobly polished guns to replace her rusty one, stuck a bowie knife in her belt instead of a tobacco pouch, attired her in one of the cream-white Stetsons and the immaculate flamboyance of buckskin, put her on an Indian pony groomed like an Arabian thoroughbred, and were off.

They must have ridden slowly, as became a business expedition that was also a pageant, for the news of their approach reached Deadwood before them. On the last slope down into the gulch the populace met them. The miners roared their boisterous delight as though welcoming a president or a burlesque troupe. Veterans of Kansas and Wyoming gaming tables and saloon fights fought for places within range of Mr. Hickock's prodigious hand-shaking reach, claiming greetings from eminence with yells of—"Bill, don't you remember me when—?"

Californians and Nevadans new to these diggings, rival gamblers and would-be rival killers, thugs fearing a new city marshal of deadly accuracy, solid citizens desiring one, appraised the famous stranger with dry curiosity. Tenderfeet on the outskirts of the crowd shuddered deliciously to meet this idol and allegory of dreadfulness face to face. Women of the town screamed and wheezed with ecstatic curiosities and bawdy enticements to greatness.

Down the rutty trail they streamed into the raw settlement, a frenzied milling of dust, exaltation, envy, admiration, spree psychology. Suddenly they were aware of Calamity. By hundreds they knew her and she knew them: gray-streaked, hump-shouldered miners she had not seen since she was the little wildcat of Blackfoot Gulch, Montana; tie-choppers, section hands, discharged soldiers from the old Wyoming and railroad days now turned prospectors, stockmen, bar-tenders, whatever was

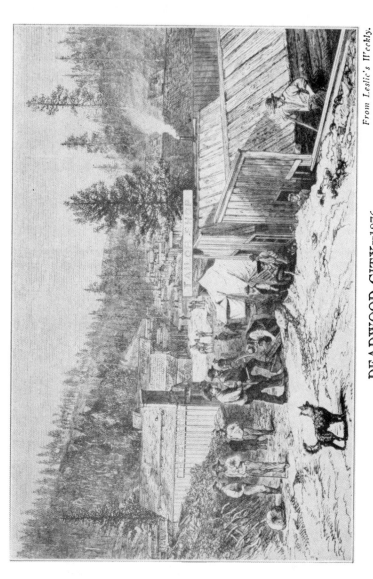

From Leslie's Weekly.

DEADWOOD CITY—1876

Where Wild Bill and Calamity Jane First Made Main Street Famous

pleasant to their horny hands; gamblers from luxurious Salt Lake City, pimps from Kansas; cow-boys retired from the trail for gold-digging or a little rustling for mining camp profits; saloon magnates who had enjoyed her patronage in the construction camps and the cow-towns; dance-house girls with whom she had fought for the more charming and harder-spending raw-hiders and would fight again; bull-whackers with hundreds and thousands of miles of her traveling company to remember; sentimentalists looking to realize their dreams of the "prairie queen" or of one of Mr. Beadle's heroines in mature loveliness.

"Calamity, Calamity!" they roared in approbation. "Hey, Calam, you remember me?"

She expanded under it, she grew florid, she scorned Mr. Hickock's grim dignities as the mannerisms of a cod-fish. She screamed, she exulted, she waved her arms and leaned over from the saddle to bestow enormous hugs and buffets. It was her triumph, she was attached to greatness. For the moment she was more exciting, more effectively responsive to this blissful adulation than greatness itself.

In a life devoted to distinction as she appraised it, this was the supreme afternoon.

And like a happy hysteric she mouthed her wild bacchanal endlessly, regally, wildly, in a frenzy of bussing and delight.

"Hello, you sons of mavericks, when are you going to buy the drinks?"

They bought them. They bought in dozens, eventually in hundreds. Ladies who would not have recognized Miss Canary socially were enduring ostracism, scorn and ridicule less than two thousand miles away by preaching that women had the same inalienable rights as men. Miss Canary had never heard of them, and would have been amused if she had.

She was a man among men and what was the use talking about what was simply a matter of meeting the boys on their own ground and doing as you damn pleased? That night she celebrated her woman's rights festival by getting tight as a goat.

For five weeks she wandered in the wake of eminence. Mr. Hickock quickly doffed his circus costume for the dignified Prince Albert of a working gambler but Jane trotted after him in her engaging buckskin, rapidly fraying from hard travel and staining from saloon usage. It was good to be Calamity Jane on your own account, but it was better still to be the recognized, even if condescendingly recognized, walking companion of Wild Bill. For one thing it gave you a chance to crow over the dance-house hussies,—as Charlotte had crowed over the farm wives of Princeton. For another, it increased the milling of men about you. Some came to seek your favors or to be amused by your grotesque swaggering and some came to admire Mr. Hickock. It made no difference. The more the merrier.

I find no evidence, however, that Mr. Hickock's attitude was more than one of genial tolerance. The best of the mining camp beauty was his for the asking, and the gentleman was fastidious. Calamity's charms were still in a state in which they were presentable when they got a good scrubbing. But they were already noticeably less than those of the newer vintage of dance-house queens, and the scrubbings were rarer than formerly.

Mr. Hickock, even if not restrained by his recent marriage vows, could hardly have been bowled over by them. So, although an occasional Deadwood ancient hints sinisterly of scandal to satisfy old grudges, the plausibilities are that he merely regarded Calamity as a profitable affliction. She had played her part well in his extravaganza, and he owed her something. If she cared to bask in the reflections of his glory, walk down the street with him arm in arm, exchange drinking courtesies with him, greet him with ostentatious familiarity, he knew how to pay a debt graciously.

But they occupied separate establishments. When they were seen together, it was invariably in the most definitely public assemblages when sentimental passages were ruled out by the code. If he ever at all enjoyed her favors, it must thus have been in the secrecy which his reputation for exquisite tastes demanded; it was done out of gratitude rather than interest and with a polished but definitely Olympian condescension. Calamity herself, though more and more grossly given to over-statements, insisted always afterwards that their relations were strictly Platonic.

But certainly no more plausible is the theory that Mr. Hickock's presence inspired her to a brief effort at moral regeneration by which she proposed to make herself worthy of his friendship. On the contrary, she seems to have devoted herself with peculiar intensity to the heroic task of shocking Deadwood.

The effort must have been prodigious. From California to Kansas the men, and not a few of the women, in the gulch's population had spent twenty-seven years acquiring the sophistication, the trickeries, the ostentations of western depravity. Post-graduates in murder, mayhem, card sharpery, bar-room bullying, liquor consumption, brothel technique, they came here from the mining gulches, the cow-towns, the army posts to flaunt what they had, to outshine each other and, when it was still possible, learn from each other. The gulch town in many ways represented the old, bawdy west at its flowering. Ten years before, even at Virginia City, it still had something to learn. Ten years later, it would have begun, what with the mortality of its experienced veterans and the rising pressure of law and the conventions, to forget.

Nevertheless, Calamity scored. Other women of her class squawled and clawed each other over lovers and customers, sometimes mauled their men in fits of drunken jealousy. But Calamity began to be famous for the fights she picked with men in a spirit of berserk delight. One night just in time to prevent possibly historic casualties, she and a newly arrived cowboy were pulled apart as they circled around each other with drawn bowie knives. A little later, when the usual friendly explanations were made, the young man's inebriacy was almost as much shocked as his Texan chivalry to learn that his antagonist was a woman. A bar-tender, attempting to quell a rough-house with which she was disturbing the pastoral peace of his establishment, was tapped into blissful insensibility by a stove-log in her lady-like hand, and the disturbance went pleasantly on.

She led the field in grotesque wildness as well as in feminine violence. An evening visitor in one of the town's leading bagnios— she appears never to have been an inmate of these establishments except at the lowest ebb in her fortunes—she had to be locked in a closet by the proprietress for language offensive to the house's standards of decorum. Once with a crowd of cheering revellers at her heels and equipped with attachments to disguise her sex more efficaciously than usual, she made the rounds of the Chinatown dives, and collected a sizeable bet that the Chinese Cyprians would not recognize one of their sisters. She began to sound the town's most famous code of practical philosophy. She would never again go to bed sober or with a penny in her pockets. No evidence survives to indicate that she was unfaithful to her trust.

What Mr. Hickock thought of his protégée is buried in the reticence of his thoughtful consideration for all "ladies." But Mr. Hickock's opinion was not long to be of current consequence. Wild Bill had reached a position where he was fatally attractive to the inferiority sense of would-be desperadoes. On August 2, a youth named Jack McCall, six years out from Louisville, and with a reputation to make for being a bad man in a bad town, shot Mr. Hickock through the back of the skull in Nuttall and Mann's gambling parlors, messily but effectively.

The garrulity of the older Calamity has surrounded this epic catastrophe with a haze of tradition. The broken-hearted mistress, the regenerated tough, the enraged lioness of a thwarted Platonic friendship, the resourceful plains scout (take your choice) cornered the murderer in a butcher's shop with a meat cleaver and captured him. In her righteous wrath she remembered having turned the wretch loose once before when she had the drop on him at a stage-robbery, and reminded him with dime novel sententiousness: "I give ye your life oncet. I'll take it back now." Or, if you prefer her as the Deadwood vigilante's heroine, she uttered this melodramatic sentiment while pulling the rope at the lynching.

Unfortunately for romantics, the whole business is typical Calamity balderdash. There was no lynching. A miners' court, somewhat relieved to be rid of the peril of Mr. Hickock's presence, promptly acquitted McCall on his plea that Wild Bill had similarly assassinated his brother in Kansas. There is not the slightest indication in Black Hills gossip or record that either McCall or Calamity had ever been present at a stage robbery. But half an hour after the murder, while McCall was really being captured, Calamity, in feminine costume as befitted a strictly emotional spectacle, sat by the body of the giant in Nuttall and Mann's howling her grief in impressively alcoholic quavers.

She knew the worth of her slight contact with greatness and what was due it. She had intimations, no doubt, that without this mighty patronage her celebrity would lose some of its luster, and so she genuinely grieved that the contact was over. But I doubt if she ever forgot for an instant that the place where Wild Bill's body was was also the place where men would congregate to console and be sympathetic,—and buy drinks.

The skids were under her now. She was never to be the "Prairie Queen" again, or the rough and tumble belle of bull trains and construction camps, or the rowdy but exhilarating scandal of marching regiments. In out-of-the-way spots the western scene was to endure another dozen years as a reality, and still another twenty-five as a pageant. But she was not to ride again down its uproarious gulches in the gorgeous company of its master showmen.

From a delectable novelty, a vivid and genial allegory of an era's hearty rowdiness, she would pass down-grade to become a jovial sot, the feminine equivalent of an old King Cole of the roistering western underworlds, the focus of a thousand meaty sagas and traditions, a hag of Rabelaisian glamor and burlesque eccentricities. From a celebrity she sank to a "character," tolerated mainly for the sake of the condescending amusement she afforded, and not a little, I fear, of a public nuisance.

Yet the rest of her life is a curious, ironically refreshing, mixture of climax and anticlimax. Deadwood, Lead, Cheyenne, Billings, Livingston, Rawlins, Rapid City—her own people in a dozen communities along her established circuits accepted her simply as a peculiarly engaging type of town bum, an exceptionally prolific source of questionable humor. They were no more impressed with the scouting and Indian-fighting stories than if she had told them she wrote the novels signed by William Dean Howells. The country thronged with discharged soldiers of the Indian campaigns and retired bull-whackers who knew her record, and they were not a people to be impressed with talk.

But as she shrank into a regional "character" at home, her fame grew everywhere else. As early as 1878, she had imposed on one Horatio N. Maguire, or Mr. Maguire imposed on his public, to include her scouting saga in a book of pretentiously serious western observations. *The Coming of Empire* it was entitled and Calamity was given a piquant place among the empire-builders. The engraved portrait of "Miss Martha Canary, the Female Scout"

Photo Elmer & Co. Boston –

Courtesy of the Historical Society of Montana.
From "The Coming of Empire" by Horatio N. Maguire.

CALAMITY JANE

The Beautiful White Devil of the Yellowstone

stares from horse-back across the sun-drenched prairies, scanning the land for Indians with the uncanny intentness of Kit Carson. The paragraphs celebrating her scalping and scouting performances are shadowy in their indefiniteness, but they convey no doubts. And to place her definitely in the western category, the tradition is sponsored that at the business end of a shooting iron she had recently made "an editor" (location uncited) retract his charges of her being a "horsethief, a highwaywoman, a three-card monte sharp and a minister's daughter."

But *The Coming of Empire* was only an introduction. Dime novels blossomed out into fictional but nominally "true confessional" accounts of her prowess under such titles as *The Beautiful White Devil of the Yellowstone*. Magazines with western interests took her up, exploited her as sober history, and still do. Talented young women in the east and even in England grasped their pens in a tremble of feminist admiration and wrote of her career, both factitiously and fictitiously, as establishing a new notch in womanly achievement. An English magazine wrote of her in a tone of solid British decorum, referring to the place

of her unfortunate confinement in Butte as
"the gaol."

Up and down the continent newspaper clip-
pings fluttered her fame by hundreds, no doubt
by thousands. Even in the summer of 1927
the astonishing legend once more awoke and
flourished in the wake of Mr. Coolidge's
Black Hills vacation. Most of it was invented
after the more thoroughly colorful period of
her life was lived, and some of it is definitely
posthumous. Actually, since I have begun
this paragraph an account dated 1917 has
reached me, certified to be on creditable authority, that she "owned" the saloon in which
Wild Bill was killed.

Nobody with first-hand knowledge of her
career took this lore seriously except in its
pornographic phases, and yet it continued to
spread. How account for it? I believe the
main explanation is twofold: that the west was
becoming conscious of itself as a lurid spectacle; and the less lurid it became in reality,
the more pleasure it took in hoaxing tenderfeet.

Deadwood itself was a mining camp opened
to the full accompaniment of a "human interest" press battery. In its first two years it

appears to have been visited by the more competent heart throb correspondents of half the metropolitan newspapers in the republic, and of the *London Times* as well. Young residents with an itch to describe the rococo found a fairly constant market for whatever made the west seem boisterous, wicked, unkemptly joyous, dangerous. Tenderfeet in droves came there, with no professional writing connections, but with a yearning to meet typical Bret Harte or Beadle novel characters and describe them minutely to the people back home in voluminous letters. Drummers, bar-tenders, gamblers and hangers-on came, happy to acquire a new stock of "typically western" anecdotes that would amaze their patrons and chance companions in more civilized and less accurately informed regions.

Already Mr. Hickock, the "poet scout" Jack Crawford and Buffalo Bill with his agreeable mountebankery had capitalized this interest in their winter theatrical appearances. The day of the wild west show was drawing near. In the public prints, on the lecture platform and in the eastern American's stock of time-passing conversation, it had already opened. As for Deadwood itself, the town's malignly insinuating name gave a fillip in the headline accounts of desperate deeds and to accounts of any piece of picaresque or brutal violence that might flow down the stream of national gossip from anywhere. Nor was its reputation for marvels lessened by the fact that Wild Bill was killed there and that between April 1877 and March 1878 it enjoyed eighteen homicides.

In the town's famous years few seekers for representative romantic features arrived without encountering Calamity in the first few hours. Except for a few bull-whacking trips to Pierre and Sidney and still briefer prowls through the Black Hills towns she seems to have been attached almost as firmly as a permanent resident. In an age when Dr. Mary Walker's trousers were still a national scandal, the sight of a woman in man's dress drinking at the bars, playing at the tables, cracking a bull-whacker's whip or firing off guns for a street crowd's diversion, was warranted to have on all but the incurably shock-proof tenderfeet a positively electric effect.

The visitor took one horrified look at the apparition and demanded of the nearest available local authority: "My God, what's that?"

And the west, to its credit, satisfied him. The old-timers gathered around, as if on a fire signal, from old-timers of two days' standing to old-timers of twenty years.

"That's the woman who killed Crazy Horse," they would barrage his ignorance. "Sure and she was the last scout to get away from Custer before the massacre." "That gal, I tell you, has a belt at home with more than forty Sioux scalps to it." "The only woman who helped build the Union Pacific . . ." "She helped Wild Bill clean up Abilene." "The handiest man with a gun in the whole west now that Wild Bill's dead . . ." "Sure, she's a regular guard on the Cheyenne treasure coach. Just layin' off this week for a little vacation." "Best scout the Indian army ever had, been in it since the Civil War, I guess." "You'd just otta have seen her the night the road agents held up the stage from Cheyenne and Johnny Slaughter got killed. Didn't she clean up them roughs with her two guns and pick up them reins and drive into town clean as a whistle?" "You bet, she was Wild Bill's woman, an' a fit one at that." "The hell you say some other Indians killed Crazy Horse! Wasn't I there and seen with my own eyes?" "Look-a-here, you look like a sensible young feller. But you pilgrims can't expect to git along in this country until you stand in better with prominent citizens like Calamity Jane."

At this point Calamity herself would be brought into the proceedings, admit all and with a hard look at the offensive ignoramus proceed to add elaborations. Or she would contribute a grin of mildly alcoholic candor and advise that he was to pay no attention to the "damn lies of them joshers," but the real question was, who was going to buy a drink? In the one case the news letter or the personal correspondence which left Deadwood on the next eastern mail would refer to the plains heroine's "calm pride in harsh duties accomplished in spite of her woman-nature's horror of violence and bloodshed." In the other, due tribute would be paid to her "gruff pioneer modesty—refreshing as a true man's."

But invariably, whatever might be Calamity's mannerism of the moment, the stories were sent, and the hoax went on. Visiting editors, with the pompous aloofness which the era's extravagant regard encouraged, sent them and went back, knowing no better. Younger

Courtesy of the Historical Society of Montana.
Taken in Gilt Edge, Montana, in 1897 or 1898.

CALAMITY JANE

reporters learned the truth after a day or two of subterranean observations, but sent them anyway, needing the space pay. In time the western towns themselves produced a whole corps of journalistic neophytes who were introduced to outside correspondence perquisites by the discovery that Calamity was likely to be good for a few sticks back east, any time, absent or present.

Old-timers related her prowess so often for the benefit of astounded strangers that they themselves forgot how to separate fact from fiction. Later comers of the early '80's who became old-timers in due course themselves, took the lore of her early activities as western gospel and circulated it with utter sincerity. Two hundred miles from her current stamping ground more performances would be invented for her as time went on, and had for their auditors and circulators all the validity of tribal folk lore for primitives.

A young graduate of the university of Michigan and the Columbia Law School was going west on the Union Pacific in 1879 to enter practice in San Francisco. In the smoker a strong, weather-beaten woman with a cowboy hat and coarse riding skirt came and shared the seat with him. She lit a pipe and asked him his business. He told her.

"Now what the hell do you think of that?" she argued pleasantly. "Going to San Francisco when the town's already gone to the business damnation, and he might be coming to Deadwood!"

"Now, look-a-here young fellow," she admonished him, "you look honest and smart. You come on up to Deadwood with me, and start practicin' and if there ain't enough law business to begin with I'll make it for you."

The youth politely rejected the invitation and was told without rancor that he would regret it. On the way back to his Pullman, he asked the conductor what might be the nature of the female who smoked a pipe, cursed publicly, and corralled strange young men for Deadwood law chambers.

"Why, that's Calamity Jane," came the answer, "and while it's none of my business, you could do lots worse than do as she tells you. That old girl has scouted with Custer, made a gold strike in the Black Hills and owns half the saloons and dance halls in Deadwood right now, to say nothing of being the boss of Black Hills politics."

The conductor had been on the line, my informant tells me, only a year himself. Quite possibly he believed every word of it.

Obviously she enjoyed it more than a little, but seldom, I think offensively. She appears to have bragged less of her scouting performances in later years when the towns were full of thrill-seekers pining for it than in the days when every army post thronged with soldiers who knew what the exact nature of her military adventuring was. Often she treated the subject with a coy reticence, and sometimes with positive denials.

No doubt she found it more amusing, and simpler, to let her fame grow of its own force. With her insatiable appetite for notice, especially male notice, celebrity was necessary no matter how she got it. But her outcast's whimsical contempt for the standard social values and precedences made her peculiarly relish a celebrity that came without any need to look the part or deserve it. Charlotte had shocked the Mercer county proprieties by being at once a farm wife and beautiful, at once a beauty and a "hell cat." How much sweeter for Martha Jane to shock the rising

proprieties of a west ardently seeking the refinements and the restraints of convention, by
being at the same time nationally famous and
the regional vagabond. Such contrasts rendered the dish doubly delicious.

Even so, she heaped high the seasoning. It
began in the very month of Mr. Hickock's
fatality when she rode one night with Colorado Charlie and Bloody Dick Seymour on
their mail route, a private business enterprise,
both spectacular and lucrative, from Deadwood to Custer City. That was material for
the legend that the slim frontier girl, with
her Indian craft, her Yankee daring and her
trusty rifle across her knees, had carried the
government mails over Sioux-infested mountain trails and bandit-haunted gulches.

One morning in the spring of '77, she rode
out of the mists,—one fears from an amorous
prospector's cabin,—near the village of Spearfish on the Black Hills northern outskirts.
There she informed a grateful wagon train
boss that the Indians had murdered a family
near the northwestern trail and they had better look out for ambushes. No Indians appeared but the gossip of the outland tragedy
proved authentic. Hence the lore manipu-

lators credited her with a lone scouting trip which saved the entire Black Hills population from massacre.

That same spring Johnny Slaughter, famed as the most efficient and charming of Cheyenne stage drivers, was killed by the fire of some hasty road agents. Dropping in from one of her mountain rambles shortly after the stage arrived and telling tall tales with mysterious unction, Miss Canary got credit with certain local romanticists and practical jokers for having stopped the run-away, seized the reins from the dead driver's hand and driven the team into the outskirts of Deadwood. Even the long survival of one Iler, who actually did perform this, and of various passengers who witnessed it, did not succeed in dimming the luster of this fantasy east of the Missouri.

Fame, too, needed a certain nobleness to bolster it, and it was supplied, I think, somewhat more veraciously. Living a strictly male life of hygienic abandon varying from a careless housekeeping to gross dirt, the miners were a constant prey to epidemics. "Mountain fever," typhoid in its various forms and degrees, ravaged them every summer and autumn. Winters came small-pox and in 1878

the South Dakota mines and freighting camps
endured a peculiarly virulent onset of "black
diphtheria." Calamity, who had no more
fear of contagions than she had of town marshals or powerful liquors, dropped her town
vices on each occasion and went nursing.

It is difficult to discover the exact extent of
her rôle as the gulch's angel of mercy, but
whatever it was, its results were intensive emotionally. Among dozens of her surviving contemporaries I could find but one able, out of
either positive knowledge or credible hearsay,
to remember the name of a single beneficiary
of her attentions. Yet almost invariably the
west gives her credit for having saved hundreds, with all the harrowing details one wants
provided one will accept them vague.

She straightened out filthy cabins, it is said,
comforted the dying, bathed the feverish, ap-
plied ointments, wrote last letters to relatives,
gave medicines, cooked invalids' delicacies,—
did all, in fact, that contemporary medicine required except to take temperatures. Undoubtedly she aided convalescents with the conventional stimulants. Also, and by this time no
doubt inevitably, she created more legends.

During one of these epidemics, her epic has

it, a new store proprietor sold a hard-looking female an assortment of groceries and preserved delicacies that would have kept a fair-sized family through a Montana winter. He helped her wedge her treasures into a capacious burlap sack and throw it over her sturdy shoulders. Then he bent over his counter to make the addition. When he looked up he was facing down the muzzle of a steadily pointed six-shooter and a sinister contralto thunder was rolling about his ears.

"I'm Calamity Jane, by God, and them sick boys I'm lookin' out for up in the hills don't pay for no grub till they get good and able. Get that?" As she vanished through the door with the approved backing-out step of the successful stick-up artists, amused by-standers convinced him that to attempt prosecution under the circumstances would be a dangerously anti-social manœuver.

Nor were her Robin Hood charities, by the lore's version, exclusively directed toward relieving masculine distress. At this same period she was brought before a peace justice for "rolling" a befuddled stranger in a dance house for the tidy sum of thirty dollars. She confessed the offense genially, but explained that the thirty was needed to send a sick girl in the establishment to the hospital. She was discharged with the court's apologies.

These are appealing tales and certainly not out of key with her taste for flamboyance even in the virtues. Yet it may be significant that in a country where much is still remembered of her concretely, one found it impossible to locate an old-timer who could vouch for them either on his own authority or the personal knowledge of a witness. Both are located with great positiveness by the ready believers in Deadwood, Livingston, Custer,—half a dozen towns. Yet both belong to the "they say" category exclusively.

One can only hope that they have more basis than the claim of a leading Black Hills anti-traditionalist that all her nursing exploits amounted to was "taking a little whiskey to the boys now and then when she had more than she could put away herself." The main point, perhaps, is that her eccentricities had taken such a hold on the local imagination that she could not perform the least kindness without becoming an allegory of heroic generosities.

So it was, too, with her erotic adventures.

She was not, it seems fairly well agreed by her contemporaries, partial to the frantic and simultaneous promiscuities of common Cyprians. While there were occasional lapses due to the claims of charming rivals and her financial difficulties, she evidently preferred one man at a time when she could get him, even though the time might be of the briefest. It is a fair question if she was ever legally married, since if she had been her divorce record would have been memorable even to the present generation. Nevertheless, between the mythical Lieutenant Somers and the handsome young one-legged hack-driver, Burke, who definitely survived her, there flourished an imposing list of men who passed as her husbands. Allegheny Dick of the Kansas days perhaps did not belong to it, since his relations were officially paternal. But there was a Hunt, a White, a Blake and possibly a Dalton. There was the tie-chopper of the Laramie neighborhood, a nameless logger she "married" on Bald Mountain near Deadwood in '77, a bull-whacker on the trails between Rawlins and Lander in the early '80s, a drunken painter in Livingston, and surely Sergeant Siechrist. There was, if you wished to believe his most earnest detractors and slight his bonds with Madame Lake Hickock of the circus, Wild Bill.

So the west made, after its dime novel self-glorifying fashion, a full rounded story out of it. She had—it was only for spoil-sports to count them and ask questions—exactly twelve husbands and of these exactly eleven, all but the curiously immortal Mr. Burke, met violent deaths within a few weeks of their nuptials. Why not? If you wanted reasons for calling her Calamity, here was another one.

The Joan of Arc of the Indian wars, the angel of mining camp mercies, the tragic bearer of an erotic nemesis, the imp spirit of the frontier's female wildness—she was becoming folk lore. If she had lived a quarter of a century earlier while the west was less literate and more a prey to word-of-mouth legends, if she had been seen by less people and had remained a legend to more, if she had haunted Bent's Fort and the wilder Nevada canyons instead of towns already predestined to Rotary and some symptoms of the historical conscience, she might have become all that *The Beautiful White Devil of the Yellowstone* represented her to be, and a lady Paul Bunyan besides.

But she was getting old. The life of brawling, exposure, constant potations was affecting
her looks, her vital instinct for lurid adventure
if not her extraordinary hardiness. When she
rode with Wild Bill into Deadwood in '76, she
still had the bold swagger and much of the
beauty of youth. In 1879 when the young
lawyer from Columbia met her on the Union
Pacific, she was only twenty-seven, or at most
twenty-eight, to his twenty-four. Yet he supposed her to be, as he puts it when he works
back to his youthful viewpoint, "an old woman
of forty-five or so."

More, the life which had given her scope for
her peculiar flamboyance was passing. Except
in remote Arizona there were no Indians for
her to ride against with the cavalry's bull trains
after 1877. New railroads were still to be
built, but by steady workmen, mainly foreigners, rather than by riotous adventurers.
There were to be new mine strikes after Deadwood but the railroads and an active police force
would push in immediately in the wake of the
first lucky prospectors. And even when the
old life did flare up momentarily at Leadville,
Cripple Creek or the Kingston, New Mexico,
diggings, she did not plunge toward it with the

barbaric energy with which she had invaded Deadwood and the railway camps.

She was growing a little sodden, bound to her little round of increasingly dull north-western towns where she knew her families would be—and free drinks . . . A hazy alcoholic comfort surrounded her, the region's mocking but pleasant respect for her mock celebrity, the hearty, back-slapping fellowship of bar-rooms and "houses." What was the use of going where you had to build this up all over again? If it was change you wanted, there was change enough between Rawlins and Livingston, between Billings and Rapid City, where, gratefully enough, all these really essential conditions were the same. There were still bull trains to ride with, or, in affluence, a cannon-ball stage coach with the cheerful company of the joshing guards. Or there were the railways where the conductor who would put you off for not having the fare to where you were going,—or any fare at all, for that matter,—would be a regional monstrosity.

So she travelled, and had now, for celebrity, only her grotesqueries to fall back on. One catches sight of her now only in rare glimpses of this quality. Men would see her for years, almost daily, and only remember her by the high points of her social blasphemies.

She joined a troupe of mining camp burlesque artists known as Al Sweringer's "Lady Entertainers." But even this agreeably loose profession had its conventions in the late '70s and she was dismissed, so the report goes, for improvising lines and postures beyond the "limit," also for appearing at a series of Deadwood performances impossibly drunk. To Mr. Sweringer, no doubt, burlesque was a serious business and he could tolerate no actress, however valuable to the publicity side, who insisted on burlesquing it.

Montana and Wyoming claimed her for the greater part of the '80s. When the town of Billings consisted of a Northern Pacific construction camp, a store or two, and half a dozen saloons with apartments above them for ladies of temporary attachments, a traveler who knew her observed her leaning out an upper window and cursing a defaulting teamster. Her expert virulence had drawn a cheering crowd and even now stands out as memorable in the observer's fifty years of profane western memories. Livingston remembers her being thrown bodily out of a house of peculiarly riotous fame for

drawing two guns on its guests one summer
night and making them "dance tenderfoot."
Miles City remembers her for shooting the
elegant mirrors out of the town's newest saloon,
while the German bar-tender who would not
serve her a drink received racial compliments
which might profitably have been preserved
for the late war's official billingsgate in bayonet
practice.

Rawlins, Wyoming, remembers her for having all but stampeded a bull train with an attack, possibly real but probably simulated, of
delirium tremens. She kept a prankish wit
about her for these excitements which expressed
itself in words at times, as effectively, as in
actions. A cattle driving outfit in central
Wyoming in the middle '80s camped for noon
dinner opposite a station consisting of one water
tank and one saloon on a railroad. Out of the
saloon Calamity wandered and, making a bee-
line for the chuck wagon, without either asking
favors or awaiting an invitation, began helping
herself to the refreshments.

The owner of the herd, a personage aspiring
to afflict the west with eastern proprieties, rode
in a surrey and was clad in the height of Cheyenne's best tailoring fashions. Sitting a little

apart from his men, he looked at the guest snappishly over his glasses and gave the trail boss a low-toned but generally audible order to fire her out.

Calamity grinned cheerfully at the cowboys, and inquired, "Boys, who's the distinguished dirty dog you're feeding that nice chow to?"

That was enough, for she had the gift of inflicting social humiliations. The general shout of laughter that went up made the owner retreat a little further into resentful aloofness while the trail boss sat down with a wink and the cook heaped her plate with a second helping of beans.

When the new town of Casper began to thrive wildly in the early '90s, her ever present urge to fight constables had developed into an obsession. One night at least she went to jail at the business end of a lariat. But Deadwood, apparently, lacked this safety-first technique of cow-craft. Hence one midnight, probably in 1893, they took the town marshal home in a wheelbarrow, comfortably sleeping off the effects of a brilliant crash from a stove-log, while a cheering crowd stayed up to buy her more drinks.

The plains were mostly out of her scheme

now, since one could ride almost anywhere on the railroads. But she must have felt with satisfaction on the whole that for a town life this was pretty good, the kind she had wanted to live ever since the Virginia City days; gaily contemptuous of the milk and water regulations of "nice people," of the "lady-like" little girls of Princeton and its solemn, joy-killing deacons; spectacularly, but not quite harmfully, ferocious; above all, the kind of an existence that made people know you were still alive.'

Dimly, too, amid the whiskey fumes, she must have recognized that there was a certain technique for such an existence. Those eastern tourists expected in a lady wildcat conduct becoming of the species, and she satisfied them. And for her western contemporaries, these smug, respectable ex-roisterers and hellions who had retired into bank presidencies, Y.M. C.A. directorships, company manners and cowtown elegancies, what more cheerful way could be found of putting them in their places than by parodying their artificial refinement with this open, abandoned recklessness? What could more wholesomely abase their present bland self-righteousness than to remind them

now and then by some publicly blatant familiarity of the old life and associations?

Let them climb all they pleased and entertain visiting bishops and congressmen as it
suited them. For an honest old rounder, what
social triumph could beat meeting a certain
Black Hills moral patriarch on the street, and
watching the crowd gather while he lectured
you unctuously on the need of mending your
ways before the Day of Judgment?

For his climax she had her sledge-hammer
memories to crush him with. "Aw, you go to
hell, Hank," she would say veraciously. "I
don't take my preachin' from an old goat I've
slept under the same blanket with more'n a
hundred times." With that off her chest she
could relax and enjoy the jovial spectacle of a
Methodist elder carried off to buy drinks for
the crowd.

The old west had become a career open to
talents. Dead as a reality, it went into the wild
west show business. Buffalo Bill flourished and
half a dozen rivals more or less profitably imi-
tated. But Calamity was out of it. Shooting
up stage-coaches on the circus grounds might be

very well, but who wanted a lady performer who was capable of shooting up saloons and beating up policemen in a nice town with two hundred and fifty years of decorum behind it, a town, say, like Springfield, Massachusetts? Besides, her trick shooting was more of a myth than ever now her hands were trembly from liquor.

Still, there was celebrity going to waste and the show world might be cheating itself not to capitalize it. The dime museums at last swallowed misgivings and took the speculative risk. She might be a little uncertain in her appearances and the management would doubtless have to keep a bail and damage fund on hand. Still she might draw enough trade to cover the investment. Even when she did happen to be incapacitated, the human skeleton and the fat lady could be trusted to be on hand because of alcohol's intolerable effects on their metabolism. The two-headed boy and the wild man from Sumatra would be in their cages because they didn't know enough to drink.

Early in 1896, once more in immaculate buckskins and with two highly polished guns on her hip, she invaded the Palace Museum at Minneapolis. Chicago, St. Louis, Kansas City and the way stations saw weather-beaten features and a hawk-eyed glance appropriate to an Indian-killer and were delighted. The autobiography was printed and proved satisfyingly impressive. So was the brief lecture on her career which she learned to pronounce, eastern words and all, when the barker paused at her platform. Mornings off, she lounged about the swanky hotel lobbies of the mauve decade, the admiration of young drummers, with airs of appropriately aloof ferocity. She learned to carry liquor on her hip and no longer to punish Palmer House bar-tenders for not extending to her weaker sex the courtesies of Deadwood.

She told taller tales than ever of her western exploits and informed old Black Hills friends magnificently, at chance encounters in the cities, that she was making $500.00 a week, which was probably not more than ten times exaggerated and certainly not more than twenty times. At any rate, it was the high water mark of her prosperity and she swanked large bills about in much the same spirit in which Charlotte had flaunted her naughtiness. A Black Hills social leader, horrified to discover her lingering about her door at the Palmer House in a condition of advanced inebriacy, courageously took her in and bought her a slight collation. She had to restrain her almost by main force from paying for a seventy-five cent meal with a ten dollar bill and giving the waiter the change.

With the summer of 1901 came the climax of this magnificence. A Midway outfit claimed her services for the Pan-American Exposition at Buffalo, proposing to exhibit her exclusively. Also, surely for publicity purposes only, its prospectus set forth that it planned to reform her and make the heroine of a score of savage battlefields worthy once more of her nobler self. Spectacularly brandishing the reins of a four-horse team hitched to an old-fashioned buckboard, the heroine made her triumphal entry into Buffalo with a suspiciously red nose and suspicious protuberances, which could hardly have been extra gun-butts, on either hip.

Perhaps the reform project was simulated too veraciously, or more likely Calamity's own account is correct that there was a disagreement over her royalties on the autobiography pamphlet. In either case, the hut where the heroine was exhibited was deserted one night within a few weeks of the entry pageant, and the crowd was following Calamity to a show that was free. Drunk and fighting to the last

"Here's How!"

Courtesy of the Historical Society of Montana.
Taken in Gilt Edge, Montana, in 1897 or 1898.

"And How!"

CALAMITY JANE

gasp with the exposition officers, Calamity was shooting the Midway up.

Buffalo Bill, so the tradition goes, paid her fine and her fare back home. Though this seems difficult to substantiate, it is easy to believe. He would have, if only for the publicity there was in it.

What is certain is that before the week was out, she was back in Billings. Fresh from the train, she arrived at noon at the house of an old acquaintance of the Kansas "prairie queen" days, helped herself to dinner and borrowed ten dollars. That night, the idlers, hangers-on, pool-players, saloon customers and all other temporarily unrestricted males of the town made a sudden rush with the police force and fire department to the tenderloin.

There in the middle of the street, in the darkness of shot-out lights, stood Calamity surrounded by gaudy spurts of gunfire and a score of the town's leading heteræ in costumes ranging from conventional lingerie to not even that much. They were dancing tenderfoot, while Calamity's berserk contralto boomed after each gun-burst:

"Dance, you chippies, dance!"

It was her last night of perfect gaudiness.

They let her shoot as long as innocent by-
standers were willing to provide re-loading
services. Then gently but firmly they arrested
her and took her—home.

She drifted to Livingston, sold souvenir
portraits of herself in her scouting uniform
and panhandled for drinks, small change and
hand-outs. She grew suddenly more sottish.
A young tenderfoot writer who interviewed
her there in 1902 found that she could not
talk at all without being primed with liquor
and then could only repeat mechanically the
stilted paragraphs of the autobiography. She
was, apparently for the first time in her life,
seriously ill and spent a few weeks in the poor-
house.

In the spring of 1903 she took the road
again. In Sheridan, Wyoming, she was well
enough to enjoy a three-handed brawl with a
sheep-herder and a peace officer, and the town
paid her fare to Newcastle. Newcastle, it is
probable, paid it to Deadwood.

She came, apparently, looking for professional hospitality in an establishment for pur-
chasable frailty known as The Green Front.
The proprietess, concerned for the sex appeal

standards of her house and its 20th century decorum, had her thrown out. Shrill, chattering girls with "rats" and enormous pompadours, sleek little hussies who had never seen a bull train or a tie-chopping camp and to whom Mr. Hickock was as remote as Attila, stood in the windows and watched her hurl imprecations and a brickbat or two at the threshold. . . . Damn their fat hides, pretending they were ladies because they'd been to high school! Watch a real lady who had traveled with the kingdom of Hell on Wheels from Virginia City to Abilene show 'em.

Old friends stopped it, mercifully this time without court proceedings; the old friends whom, now that she could only think of one thing at a time, she had forgotten while she raged at The Green Front. They took her for a round of cheerful saloon visits, fed her, put her to bed, paid for her room at a congenially down-at-the-heels hotel indefinitely. They shelled out quarters, halfs, dollars, sometimes five-spots.

Old friends were getting tearily sentimental about everybody's former nobleness. Hadn't she saved the town from Indians, small-pox, black diphtheria? Sure old Calam could have their last dollar,—even if they had to borrow it. Her stock of pictures in scouting costume was replenished at the local photographer's. When these were gone, she owed him fifty dollars, but they were replenished again. Ageing rounders, exalted with the familiar beverages, young toughs seething with alcoholic curiosity, formed Bacchic routs for her escort when she made her triumphal tours of outlying towns: Spearfish; Sturgis, where she had "married" Burke, the beautiful hack-driver; Terraville; Lead City up the hill, where a canny grocer, now a bank director, closed his store against the Saturday night trade lest the invaders paw him with their booze-sticky hands and rifle his cracker-barrels in the name of this senile old home week.

Terraville somehow held her, perhaps because she forgot to go home. The first of August the driver of the stage from Deadwood saw two gray and bleary prospectors holding her up in a bar-room chair. Sick, sicker 'n all hell's fire, she groaned, and between groans chuckled that a personage of her magnificent experience should have to be fed whiskey with a spoon.

Next day there was delirium, loud chatter

of riding up the gulch with Wild Bill Hickock; about a daughter she had, or thought she had, who had been adopted by "swell people" and was the wife of a farmer away off somewhere; about wild lights, sounds, brawls, excitements, men pawing furiously over their women, that may have been Virginia City, but must have been Virginia City, Deadwood, Cheyenne, Abilene, the Overland stage stations and Charlotte's glamor all rolled into one.   In the evening she was dead. . . . Mr. Hickock's grave shade, if observant, would have smiled with the delicate grimness of gambler's humor to realize that it was the 27th anniversary of Mr. McCall's stupendous play for fame in the annals of homicide.

Deadwood, with febrile romanticism, decided that she was a part of history, and arranged a funeral gaudy as a congressman's. Also in morbid exhilaration, it attacked the glamorous carrion on the undertaker's laying out board with cameras and hair-snipping scissors until it was necessary to put a wire screen around it.

The Methodists, through the mortician's sense of obligation and through having been on the ground first to offer general condolences, won the honor of conducting the obsequies. Half the summer boarders in the Black Hills suddenly blossomed into famous soloists of metropolitan churches eager to contribute their services. The cruel stand had to be taken that this glory should only reflect locally and that the Methodist choir should sing unassisted.

The church on the great day held the grandest reunion of the rounders and the pious since the coming of the railroad; also no doubt the most pervading alcoholic fragrance in the history of Wesleyanism. In three of the most noticeable centers of this disturbance a prospector, a retired bull-whacker and a gambler respectively, bewailed audibly but not contentiously their alleged widowerhood.

Someone had remembered, or invented for her, a lifelong wish to be buried by Mr. Hickock. In carriages and on foot, stalwart and staggering, half the town streamed up the zigzag road to Mount Moriah cemetery and put her there.

A little later they gave celebrity its due in a monument—cheap, four feet high, "Mrs. Jane Burke, 53"; an appropriate memento for one so inclined to be wrong about dates and marriages.

Around its base twinkle four little gargoyle-like heads, possibly intended for cherubs but surely not, after the most celebrated Methodist funeral in Deadwood, symbols of frontier diabolism. Without art they leer genially at the doleful ravages of the souvenir hunters on a red sandstone Mr. Hickock's left arm and moustaches, and at a gaping world of tourists. Equally without art something grotesque beneath them mocked that world and sufficiently enjoyed it.

THE WOMAN HAS TO SUFFER

MR. JAMES AVERELL had an idea. He was sitting in his combination store, saloon and ranch house in the Sweetwater Valley of Wyoming when he had it, very comfortably lapped away from the early autumn frosts of 1887 by the few slugs of whiskey and the heat of his pot-bellied cast-iron stove. Between puffs of home-made cigaret smoke he leaned back in a chair and looked at the ceiling with disarming vacancy, for Mr. Averell's intellectual inspirations were often of a sort that required concealment. He even carefully remarked that a pair of loafing cowboy customers were completely absorbed in their own conversation before permitting himself a glance down his leg as though conjuring up a wrily humorous mental image at the end of its extended boot toe. Only then did Mr. Averell smile. And at that it was with such a slight narrowing of the eye slits and such a faint drawing up of the corners of a straightly cut mouth that if the cowboys had turned around suddenly they would simply have supposed that their host was resting his face from its normal poker set.

Quite evidently Mr. Averell was not so unfamiliar with ideas as to receive them with ecstatic thigh-thwacks or irresistible impulses to share the visitation with the neighbors. In fact, he had so many that he could afford to greet new ones languidly, and he used them so much in his business that giving away a good one was just like giving away capital.

There was that idea he'd had, for instance, of settling on a small homestead claim there on the Sweetwater and getting all the little squatters and discontented cowboys together under his leadership for a hell-raising agitation against the big land barons. That had paid pretty well considering he had been barely two years at it. Hadn't he won literally hundreds of followers and devoted henchmen and weren't they all his customers as well as his political supporters? Had not a grateful Democratic administration, easily impressed by agitations against Republican plutocrats, awarded him the Sweetwater post-office for his pains, which, though it didn't amount to much in itself, was certainly good for the store and saloon business?

So far so good, but more was certainly to be had by applying new ideas as they came up. For instance, Mr. Averell had had much pleasant excitement contesting the claims of his richer neighbors in the courts. He had made John Durbin prove a title, he was making a spirited nibble on the edge of Bob Connor's holdings, and it looked as if he could keep the powerful A. J. Bothwell from fencing off the rest of Sweetwater Valley. What if these annoyed land kings got together and offered a gifted and enterprising trouble-maker like Mr. Averell a respectable fortune to leave Carbon County? Or what if, as Jim Averell even more plausibly suspected, the small homesteaders were to go on increasing in numbers until, politically and otherwise, they put the big landowners in the shade? Would not the coming struggle justify an ambitious young postmaster, already an established leader of the more numerous faction, in sticking around to see what he could get out of it? By 1887, Mr. Averell had reasonably surmised that his talents had value in the community and that sooner or later he would be paid lavishly either for service, or for ceasing to serve.

Meanwhile, nevertheless, there were certain difficulties about being paid anything at all. The past two winters had been furiously destructive to cattle so that even the Wyoming land barons were disappointing as customers. Mr. Averell's particular friends, the small homesteaders, were practically bankrupt. The store and saloon did badly in spite of the post-office, and yet, simply to collect his wages as an agitator, it was necessary for Mr. Averell to hang on until times got better.

So the idea that came to Mr. Averell in the early fall of 1887 appeared to that perplexed politician very much in the light of a life-saver. And if it required using a woman to shield him in certain dangerous and highly criminal misconduct, Mr. Averell, far from being disturbed, was elated by it. He was not only shameless and ruthlessly practical in romantic matters. But, smiling craftily down his bootleg a dozen times a day during the next week or two when no one was looking, he reflected that he knew just the right woman.

Her name was Ella Watson, and although her reputation was such that no ordinary crooked promoter would have cared to use her in any enterprise whatsoever, Mr. Averell looked on that reputation as offering certain advantages. Ella Watson was a notorious loose woman of the cowtowns and for his peculiar purposes this was precisely what he needed.

There would be nothing surprising, for instance, about such a creature's coming into the Sweetwater country and setting up an establishment. The neighborhood lacked such facilities unless you counted the new, and very raw, hamlet of Casper fifty miles away. Also, the neighborhood was, even if not prosperous, excessively populated with males.

That would be explanation enough for Miss Watson's arrival, and if she should settle down near the only store and saloon on the Sweetwater, that coincidence, too, would be in nature. The new neighbor could hardly injure Mr. Averell's standing, since his followers would regard the connection between the two establishments as reasonably orthodox and since, so far as the possibly more censorious big landholders were concerned, Mr. Averell's reputation with them was no higher than a rattlesnake's already.

But once the Watson establishment was installed, Mr. Averell had no intention that it should function as a mere coincidence. It would not be enough that it should boost the business of the store and especially of the saloon more or less automatically. As the clandestine promoter of the enterprise, Mr. Averell would see to it that he shared in the direct profits. Although more or less of a professional idealist in his leadership of the small land-owners, Mr. Averell was a practical man in his business operations. When he saw an opening for profits that would tide him through the lean years of cattle depression he was proud of being able to dismiss his finer feelings entirely.

But even this prospect of a partnership was not the end of Miss Watson's economic attractions. Mr. Averell knew, as an experienced observer of the cattle industry, that one thing which the depletion of the herds and the struggle between the small and the great ranchmen were bound to produce was an increase in rustling. Cattle were scarce and proportionately valuable. Many of the small ranchers had in fact lost their herds entirely, and through a total lack of means with which to pay taxes and complete their purchase payments, were in momentary danger of losing their pastures as well. Naturally they blamed the big land-holders for this, since if these had not occupied and fenced in their ranges there would have been more pasture for the small herds and more protection from the blizzards.

Hence, many of the small ranchers felt almost conscientiously that when they rounded up a few calves or mavericks from the nabobs and used them to stave off both starvation and ejection they were merely taking something which the owners had no right to miss and were otherwise performing a civic duty by redressing the balance of economic justice. Moreover, a situation which persuaded reasonably honest ranchers that they had a moral alibi for rustling naturally attracted down-and-out cowboys, floaters, ne'er-do-wells and range criminals who needed no alibis at all and proposed to make their operations as large as possible.

Mr. Averell had been confidentially advised that he might have his share of this traffic provided he would do his part in arranging shipments and sales. Already using his position as post-master and store-keeper as a blind, he had perhaps assisted and cashed in on a few minor transactions. But for reasons flattering to his discretion, Mr. Averell was a trifle timid. A place so public as the only store and post office within fifty miles was scarcely an apt one to discuss rustling deals or to cache stolen cattle. Besides, as a moral leader of the down-and-outs, the post-master needed to preserve some shreds of outward respectability.

In order to share in the rustling proceeds on a large scale, Mr. Averell must have a blind that was plausible and safe and in the least possible degree personally incriminating.

Here was where Miss Watson came in and here was where Mr. Averell's idea was really superior. The Watson establishment, like every other place of business in a money-strapped country, would take cattle in trade. Automatically, in the normal course, it would take quite a little rustled stock. But if arrangements were perfected for marking the legitimate animals with Miss Watson's brand as fast as they were received, and then additional arrangements were made for the branding and quick dispatch of cattle that were temporarily deposited on the place by the rustlers, the Watson establishment could function admirably as a rustlers' clearing house.

Mr. Averell's connections might be suspected but it would be very difficult to prove anything. Also, it would be quite as difficult to prove anything against Miss Watson except that she was a commercial lady a little careless about exchanging cows for favors. The worst that could happen would be that now and then her corral might be raided for cattle of definite and demonstrable ownership. But even in this case the owners would blame the establishment's cowboy customers and not the woman herself. Her they would regard as a depraved town type too stupid to understand the sophisticated villainies of the open range. While they might be annoyed from time to time, their sentimental chivalry for all "ladies," good or bad, would restrain them from seriously harming her. She could probably go on for years without serious interruption and if the time ever came when she did have to leave the country, Mr. Averell could import another woman of her calling and the game would go on. Mr. Averell was making really brilliant arrangements for functioning as sales manager to the rustlers behind a woman's skirts.

So in March 1888 Miss Watson appeared, built a cabin a little less than a mile from the Averell place and filed a small homestead claim. She was a large, brunette, frowzily good-looking woman of about twenty-seven years with a sleepy brown eye which veiled more intelligence and resolution than her outward appearance suggested. Jim Averell had chosen her because she seemed to have been above the moronic giddiness of her kind and could keep her mouth shut about her dealings with the criminal classes even when in liquor. She had a little executive talent, he had discovered, for in the several small establishments she had conducted in various cowtowns and army posts, she had proved her capacity to browbeat drunken cowboys and military toughs into some semblance of orderly conduct, and had kept the authorities in their place. She was hard-boiled in emergencies and could both lie plausibly and draw a gun in a way that convinced her gentlemen that she was ready to fight.

Finally, he had chosen her because in the doting and rather pathetic fashion of her class, Ella Watson was in love with him. For Jim Averell was, when he wanted to be, a man of pleasant address and agreeable manners. His educational and social superiority to the common run of ranchers and cowboys was unescapable. In his occasional letters to the Carbon County newspapers on the land controversy, he expressed himself not only forcibly but in a

cultivated style and vocabulary. Once a visiting Episcopal rector had shocked a Cheyenne
audience by publicly boasting of having a
young Wyoming rancher and political leader,
Jim Averell, as a college class-mate. The socially exclusive and decidedly anti-agrarian
little capital knew Jim's shady reputation and
loathed his politics and the blunder was akin to
boasting at tea in some British colonial governor's drawing room that one's oldest intimate
in the place was a notorious beach comber.
Averell was obviously a rotter, an outcast, and
Wyoming respectability was convinced that he
was also a murderer and a fugitive from justice.

But he was obviously, too, on his other side,
a man of strong personal magnetism and of fair
breeding. To a woman like Ella Watson, the
product of the Kansas frontier and of the
saloon and bawdy house life of the wilder cow-
towns, he brought the glamor of culture and
social charm. And since he was hiding behind
a woman's skirts, the realistic Mr. Averell
doubtless reflected, a woman thus enamored
would be least likely to squeal.

The new establishment put itself immediately on a business basis and for a time things

went prosperously. Ella gave it out that she was accepting cattle in trade and supplied the explanation that she hoped by this means to acquire a competence soon and settle down as a ranch mistress to a life of reform and respectability.

Through a typical fancy of her kind she had recently honored a soldier admirer by changing her name to Kate Maxwell. She could hardly hope to deceive the neighborhood since everyone except the newest arrivals knew her personally as a minor celebrity in near-by red light districts. But it accepted the improvisation humorously as her symbol of an intention to become a changed woman. Indeed, in satirical tribute to her aim of attaining respectability through the cattle traffic, the countryside speedily nicknamed her Cattle Kate. Garlic by another name, the Sweetwater district sagaciously reflected, would keep the familiar smell.

There was nothing unkindly or suspicious in the attitude. To the leading citizens, the Sweetwater land barons, the establishment was simply another "hog ranch," and in the frontier spirit toward the natural depravities they tolerated "hog ranches" with jocosity rather than with moral anguish. From the first they suspected, of course, that Jim Averell had a hand in the enterprise. But this was natural enough for a saloon-keeper of the great open spaces and it was impossible to think worse of him for being a partner in a "hog ranch" than they thought of him already for being a partisan and professional trouble-maker of the little homesteaders' group.

So cows rolled in and out of Cattle Kate's corral without molestation. She was careful about it and did not encourage the appearance of excessive affluence. There were rarely as many as fifty animals grazing on her little pastures and often no more than a score. What was even more wary, but not so noticeable, was the fact that the same cows were rarely there for two weeks in succession. Every few evenings a quiet little round-up would be held and the Kate Maxwell brand affixed to the small herd of mavericks. Then in the dead of night they would be driven off toward the nearest shipping point or to one of the ranches of the little homesteaders where they could be kept in seclusion until a discreet sale could be effected.

And things prospered otherwise. In fact Mr. Averell hardly registered distress even when Mr. Harrison beat Mr. Cleveland in the autumn, and the prospect of losing the post-mastership loomed starkly before him. His campaign against the big land-holders was doubling in energy and, Mr. Averell thought, in effectiveness. "Land sharks," he was calling them now in his political conversations and letters to the Carbon County editors. All the "large tracts were so fraudulently entered" that they would have to change hands sooner or later and then "the public domain would be given to the honest settler,"—like Jim Averell and his followers. "The future land owner in Wyoming will be the people," he declared seductively, and when the "people" had real homesteading rights and water rights, you would see "orchards and farms" fill up Wyoming. Federal politics might be going against him, but Jim Averell was building himself up as a power in state politics,—which was better either for holding the whip hand or getting bought off.

The "hog ranch," too, was doing well even in those aspects from which Mr. Averell regarded it as a legitimate enterprise. Before the summer of '88 was over it was the recognized hang-out for all the rustlers, sports and hard characters for forty miles. Some customers, in fact, came from even farther when they did not, temporarily, care to show up in towns like Casper and Bessemer where there were constables and United States deputy marshals. They staged huge carousals which were infinitely better for Jim's liquor business than were stray callers at his post office. Kate often had an extra girl and sometimes two or three to assist in the entertainment. A lot of the cows that moved in and out of her corral were taken in trade quite honestly and really belonged to the customers. And the hard money that passed into the treasury was considerably more than Jim would ever have seen by selling groceries.

Still, there were danger spots. The big land-holders would have tolerated a "hog ranch" for their cowboys with amused condescension if not with more than a little paying patronage. They would not have minded its being rough and rowdy and occasionally the scene of a little gun play, since all this went with the "hog ranch" business and was, by range traditions, a regular part of the humor of life in the great open spaces.

But when the ranch became the recognized loafing place of men notoriously suspected of rustling, when these men were obviously (from their lavish expenditures) prospering better than the nabobs of the community and when the ranch itself was trading in cattle with secretive diligence, tolerance became difficult. In fact, tolerance soon passed into suspicion. By the spring of 1889, the Watson place had long been forbidden to respectable cowboys and was being casually but effectively watched. From being a sort of rustic jest at the expense of an incorrigible woman's reforming ambitions, the nickname "Cattle Kate" became a symbol of a kind of depravity for women at which a cow country did not jest at all.

Moreover, there were scandals to intensify the bitterness, scandals even for a "hog ranch." Mr. Averell's charm, such as it was, vanished with liquor and in one of the more abandoned Watson carousals early in '89 he beat a young woman inmate, tore her clothes from her and drove her out into the snow. The neighbors who found her tied to a wagon axle in the yard next morning and half dead from exposure were genuinely shocked.

Finally Mr. Averell had begun living quite openly with Ella. There is not the slightest indication that he cared any more for her than for the woman he had beaten. But if he was going to use Ella for business purposes and she was infatuated with him, Jim Averell was the sort to adapt his arrangements to keeping her in a good humor. It was not kindness and it certainly was not affection. But so long as it helped to keep Ella's place going as a rustlers' clearing house and to keep the woman herself from flying into a tantrum and giving the game away, Mr. Averell was not going to be squeamish.

Yet to the neighbors their quasi-conjugal status was another point in the evidence. They did not mind Jim Averell's being interested in a "hog ranch" and they did not mind his keeping a notorious woman. Not being articulate politicians they were not even disposed to raise the roof over the discrepancy between this part of his conduct and his sternly idealistic battle for economic justice. But when a "hog ranch" and a woman so obviously under Jim's domination were actively engaged in trading cattle which had not been definitely paid for, they felt that it was too much.

They grumbled and conspired largely in secret. But the burden of their conclusions was that a "hog ranch" should be a "hog

ranch" and a mistress a mistress, and that mix-
ing either with the Averell economic principle
that the poor had a right to take from the rich,
was a scandal worth doing something about.

Yet it was precisely when the situation began
to grow dangerous that Jim and Ella became
most reckless.   There were more reasons for
this than that Jim was drunk now most of the
time on his new prosperity and that the woman
was in love.   The great idea of Mr. Averell
was working wonderfully, and after another
disastrous winter in 1888-9, rustling operations
were increased and cattle were higher.

Also, rustling psychology was more rampant.
The small homesteaders' herds had been exterminated by the blizzards almost entirely and
replenishing them from the stock of the big
cattle barons was coming to be looked upon
almost as a moral act.   Heretofore, there had
been some slight squeamishness about being
caught with the goods.   Rustlers got off in the
county courts chiefly because the evidence
against them tended to be circumstantial.   But
late in the spring of '89 a man and his wife
were acquitted even after the hides and the
beef found on their ranch in a raid by volunteer

cattle detectives were positively identified as belonging to the plaintiff. Jim and Ella not illogically decided that no jury of typical Carbon County bankrupts would convict them even if they were surprised in the act of mavericking itself. Now, obviously, was the time to make their killing. Next winter might be less destructive and if the herds of the small ranchers ever began to increase, property would begin to sympathize with property again and the big chance would be over.

So as mavericks were scarce, they decided to extend operations. The crop of spring and fall calves were coming along, but was still unbranded. There was, however, one disadvantage about stealing calves still in the unweaned stage. Their mothers would follow them. A corral full of unbranded calves and a pasture full of bawling cows might have excited the suspicion even of an 1889 jury in Carbon County. Jim promptly resolved the difficulty by shooting the cows and driving off the calves with no followers.

June and July nights he rode the ranges with his trusted rustlers and played the new game until his saddle muscles ached. Each day the remoter grazing grounds were strewn with cow carcasses freshly killed with gun-shot. But each dawn there was a new round-up of calves at Ella Watson's. The corral, too, increased in population and frequently now, instead of two score of old range cattle, a hundred or more young stock stood in its enclosures, tasting their feed gingerly and bawling for milk and mother. But everyone of them bore Ella Watson's brand and nearly everyone of them moved often. Each night rustlers who were not out with Mr. Averell on his hunting expeditions drove them across country to the ranches of other and more passive confederates.

If they were found in these hiding places, who could prove that the little ranchers had not bought them in good faith from Ella Watson, the "common law wife" of the little ranchers' best friend? If they were found on Ella's property, she might have her difficulties, brand or no brand, in proving that they were hers by purchase; but who could prove, when the calves had no marks but hers on them and no branded mothers to follow, that they belonged to anyone else? The calves moved in and out, from Ella's to the little homesteaders, from the little homesteads to the markets, and the division of the spoils went on cheerfully. Veal after three years of herd depletion was worth almost as much as beef in normal times. The scheme seemed to be fool proof.

An angry cattle baron's foreman rode into her ranch one day in June and claimed the corral stock for his employer. Ella merely explained that she had "bought them." When he demanded proof and particulars, she announced that a lady's cattle trading operations were none of his business and ordered him off the place with a string of her best bagnio profanity. Impudence could hardly go farther, and yet it did. Rustlers on Mr. Averell's payroll, if not Mr. Averell himself, when in their cups informed cowboys and foremen of the big outfits that if their employers made any kick about the way things were going, they might expect to be shot for it.

Mr. Averell so far forgot caution that he began to invest his surplus profits in land purchases and in legitimate cattle transactions. If he had gone on a little further, he might have become a land baron himself. Cattle Kate was beginning to dress better than the women of the best families. In a country profoundly depressed in its fundamental industry, she suddenly began flaunting a fine saddle horse and a brand new buggy. Sheltered behind the class war of the plains that they had raised, protected by crooks and gunmen, sympathized with by many of their honest neighbors and equipped with a system admirably devised to baffle evidence-getters, the pair of the post office and the "hog ranch" felt that they could get away with murder.

They had forgotten only one thing, that the west was only a little way in time from the vigilante tradition and if sufficiently plagued would return to it. They had forgotten that men who boast of being above the law too openly arouse forces above the law to control them.

About the middle of July, Averell or some of his henchmen made one of their familiar calf raids on the ranch of A. H. Bothwell. It was a bigger, and apparently a bolder, raid than usual. In addition the mistake was made of taking calves which Bothwell himself, without branding or otherwise marking, had carefully noticed as the most promising of the year's crop. He knew the bunch from all the other calves in Carbon County as well as a man knows his own dogs from his neighbors'. So when he found their mothers lying shot, he went next day by the Cattle Kate ranch and identified the fifty new calves bawling in her corral, as his without question.

Bothwell acted quickly. On the morning of July 20, seven men rode up to the Watson gate, some on horse-back and some in an old-fashioned farm wagon. Six of them, the leading land-holders of the Sweetwater Valley, were furiously irritated at Averell's propaganda against their property rights and had suffered, or believed they had, from the depredations of the "hog ranch" rustlers' ring. The other was a visitor from over the mountains near Rawlins, but as a large scale rancher himself who had often been victimized by rustlers, his sympathies were entirely with his hosts. Bothwell, perhaps, dominated them because his irritation was the freshest. But things turned out as they did largely because they had no recognized leader at all.

They acted without any preliminaries. John Durbin, a pillar of the Methodist church in the county and probably the biggest land-owner in the group, broke down Ella's wire fence and drove her herd, including Bothwell's calves, out of the pasture. This took several minutes and gave Ella a chance to come up and order them off. Her first thought evidently was that the marauders were a new gang of rustlers out to apply Mr. Averell's economic theories by preying on her own prosperity.

But when she saw that her cattle were being driven off by her sworn worst enemies and that each enemy was armed both with six-shooters and the ugly look of business, her tactics changed. In her cabin she had a fresh horse if it were a question of riding, and a pretty good arsenal of her own if this was to be a shooting engagement, and she set out on a dead run for them. But Bob Connor, whose titles Averell had contested, and Earnest McLain, a rancher who had suffered heavy losses to the rustlers, had already circled in behind her and they stopped her in her tracks. Ella was a practical woman and no movie cameras were present, so there were no undignified struggles. The two men took hold of her arms and she came along as peaceably as if they were her chosen escorts.

They ordered her to get into the wagon and come to Rawlins with them. She objected a little at first but chiefly in a tone of petulant cajolery. Rawlins, she said, was a hell of a place to take a lady with only her house-work clothes on. She wanted to go to the cabin and doll up in her best. She did not, it appears, expect that men in the west would harm a woman seriously, but just as a precaution she would impress her sex upon them with this bit of feminine vanity. Having done so, she was satisfied. When her captors gave her scowlingly to understand that they were taking no chance on her ruses, she climbed into the wagon quite cheerfully.

A few minutes were spent capturing a fourteen-year-old boy who had been chasing a pony in Ella's pasture and had now caught it. The amateur vigilantes took no risk of his getting word to Averell, which, as a matter of fact, was exactly what he was planning to do. Then the little party jogged deliberately up the road to the postoffice. The woman took her situation lightly and alternately joked and cursed them with cheerful defiance.

Mr. Averell they took at a considerable disadvantage. He was just starting for Casper and had dismounted between closing the first and opening the second gate from his properties. Shut in a little enclosure too narrow for his horse to find jumping stance, he was helpless. They shouted that they had a warrant for his arrest and he had nothing else to do but to wait for them. When they came up, he asked to see the warrant. Durbin and Bothwell threw down their guns on him and told him that was warrant enough. Jim also mounted the wagon without objections.

The wagon lumbered slowly up the rutty road by the Sweetwater, two miles, three miles, four miles. In the informal western fashion its occupants wrangled, not as captors and prisoners, but as equals. What was this Rawlins trip all about? The man and the woman jawed. It was none of their business, they were answered. And there was a quarrel for almost half an hour as to whether it was any of their business or not, an exchange of angry insults that hardly left anyone in better condition for sober judgment.

Finally, the ranchmen told them. "You two have got to get out,—quit the country right now and for good. You know perfectly well why. If you don't, we'll drown you in this river right here."

Mr. Averell smiled sardonically and spat. He was a big landowner now himself, thank you,—almost a rich man. He might leave the country, of course, under certain circumstances and if it suited him. But he'd damn well be paid for it.

The woman, however, burst into wild, hysterical laughter. "Drown us in that river, like 1ell!" she screamed. "Why, there ain't enough water in that river to give one of you dirty land-hogs a decent bath."

All this was trying to the temper, and not less so since a glance at the river showed the amateur vigilantes that Ella was right. Very well, they were almost five miles from the nearest witnesses now, nearing Spring Canyon. They would take these thugs up there under one of the trees and show them how much cattle rustling paid.

The wagon was unloaded and they toiled panting over a huge mass of boulders in the creek bed, through the thick brush of the lower canyon. Ropes were suddenly produced, knotted and looped for a painful ceremony.

"All right, if drowning ain't good enough for you, maybe we've got something that is," one of the group threatened.

Averell, still hopeful, let them place the noose around his neck and took his place in the lower branches of a split cottonwood quite

jauntily. This was only a bluff, he thought
with his characteristic cynicism. The old wild
west was over and with it the old-style vigilantes. These fellows might string him up uncomfortably for a while to scare him, but they'd
end by buying him out.

But the woman by now was thoroughly ter-
rified. She fought off the noose with great
lunges of her head and torso. She clawed out
at her captors with her hands. One instant she
called down upon them a lifetime's accumula-
tion of imprecations. The next, fighting still,
she whined in loud, wheezy sobs to be spared
for the sake of their mothers and sisters.

For a lynching, even for a wholesome terror-
izing, the operation was becoming rowdy, raw,
disgusting. The tension on the nerves of the
captors was intolerable. The business must
either be gone through with or abandoned, and
at once.

Yet if there had not been an interruption at
this moment, Mr. Averell's brilliant idea might
have been paid for. But the fourteen-year-old
boy at Ella's cabin had been turned loose at
Averell's and had found the rustlers. Frank
Buchanan, a henchman of Averell's, suddenly
began peppering them with revolver bullets

from the other side of the arroyo. John Durbin dropped from a flesh-wound in the thigh.

They were amateurs and they were riled
and excited. Some of them chased Buchanan
away, harmlessly enough, with their long range
rifles. But those who stayed with the captives,
fired by impulses of terror and hysteria more
than of justice, pushed Ella and Jim out into
space.

There was no drop, and the vigilantes of the
Sweetwater Valley had not known their busi-
ness well enough to tie hands or muffle faces.
They struggled horribly for a long while.

Thirty hours later people came from Casper,
cut them down and buried them. There were
court proceedings and six of the seven men in
the hanging party were arrested. But Buchanan and two other witnesses who belonged
to Averell's little homesteaders' faction were
spirited out of the country, one of them at least,
Ralph Cole, under circumstances that pointed
plausibly to murder. Gene Crowder, the boy
messenger, died, mysteriously for a fourteen-
year-old, of Bright's disease. Conveniently
delayed for three months until these disposi-
tions could be made, the grand jury could re-

turn no indictment for lack of evidence. In a district numerically dominated by irate little homesteaders, evidence of having lynched a woman would have been awkward.

Meanwhile the Wyoming landed aristocracy, to clear itself of the scandal, invented and swallowed enormous legends of Cattle Kate's peculiar villainy. She emerged from this treatment for a time, almost heroic,—the queen of the rustlers, the brains of the desperadoes' organization and, most quaintly of all, the corrupter of Jim Averell. But too many had known her, and so to-day the super-hellcat of tradition mocks her lynchers from the grave. She was a dissolute woman foolish enough to love a crook and intelligent enough to be used by him as a pawn in some subtly criminal enterprises. But there is no reasonable doubt that if the rope which by the western code Averell richly deserved had separated her from her paramour's influence, she would have reverted to her natural harmlessness.

More than a little, too, she mocks her executioners' ferocity from the land records. A year and a half after the hanging, her ranch and Averell's were filed upon for non-payment of taxes. The little homesteader who acquired them sold them to A. J. Bothwell!

BELLE STARR

THE question of the gentility of inn-keepers mildly agitated society from the dawn of democracy down to the humbling of the Infanta Eulalia of Spain by Mrs. Potter Palmer of the Palmer House and the World's Columbian Exposition. That settled the issue, of course, the personal intervention of the lymphatic Mr. Palmer and the infant Alfonso XIII not being required, once the fray on the distaff side became decisive.

But actually the stand of the Palmer House in the controversy was only a little less conservative than the Court of Spain's. Half a century earlier the same issue had been settled in the southwestern frontier center of Carthage, Missouri, with no controversy at all. John Shirley was recognized as the first gentleman of the town of Carthage, not in spite of keeping an inn, but because tavern comforts themselves, on the edge of a wilderness, conferred social glamor.

Hill billies from the Ozarks, pioneer planters struggling with malaria and crop vicissitudes, lawyers from the lesser county seats riding circuit, jogged into its stableyard and found its architectural air of a slightly second-rate southern mansion deliciously impressive. Their appetites, jaded with surfeit of cornpone, salt pork and wild game taken in the off seasons, found in its varied fare and slightly civilized cooking unimagined heights of elegance and sensual bliss. Its fragrantly mixed liquors, after lifelong devotions to redeye and squirrel whiskey in their unadulterated virulence, conveyed startling intimations that there might be other pleasures to drinking besides getting drunk. The service and the hospitality introduced them to some of the formal graces of southern society, and, since this was done with tactful cordiality and without discouraging such established native mannerisms as tobacco-chewing and the public use of knives for toothpicks, guests expanded under the friendly urbanity in a grateful sense of having had their true worth recognized.

Farmwives and women off the covered wagons, stared with admiring envy at the toilettes which Mrs. Eliza Shirley by native talent or subscription to the current fashion magazine managed to make almost as modish as the season's offerings from Nashville and Lexington. They respected her worn but highly polished piano, however much its tones jangled in the treacherous Missouri climate, as the ultimate symbol of refined ostentation.

And there were still other reasons for this slightly feudal homage to elegance. It took more domestic slaves to run a first-rate tavern in a small metropolis than were within the means of struggling planters, needing every black arm they could afford for field work. Thus John Shirley acquired the economic respect due to splendid affluence. From having once held some minor judicial office, he had his perpetual title of "Judge," which was common enough, but he was also the intimate adviser of congressmen and state political leaders, a sort of minor boss in high matters of Democratic and extreme pro-slavery patronage. Finally, the gentleman inn-keeper was patently a scholar. Had not even his recognized intellectual equals, pioneer lawyers and preachers of the backwoods, stood in awe before the glass case with its array of novels, histories, biographies, works on philosophy and moral improvements? Literally, books by the dozen! Did not some who claimed to have counted them insist that there were more than a hundred?

Obviously, there could be no question of social standing here, or even of social leadership. Occasional Virginia slave nabobs looking for western investments, a rare Whig congressman from Boston austerely investigating slavery conditions in the border states, might insinuate class distinctions. The Arkansas border knew better. For the manners and delicacies of living it would take its cue, not from the foppish affectations of unpleasant strangers, but from the hospitable little court of good living on the Carthage Main Street.

John and Eliza Shirley presided over it for twenty-five years. One evening late in the first decade of their tenure, the slave service was slightly less organized and distinctly more excited than usual. The bar-room festivities were subdued and early concluded. The ladies' parlor succumbed to an overwhelming nervous tension and grimly excluded gentlemen visitors from its confidences. Next morning grinning black attendants solicited tips in the name of Mrs. Eliza Shirley's new daughter.

She was christened Myra Belle. The Arkansas border predicted, with a naïve pride in the enterprise's possibility, that she would be "raised for a lady." It was February 3, 1846.

In that time and place, a lady-like education emphasized ostentation rather than subtlety, mannerisms rather than manners. Being accomplished was so much of a rarity that it hardly seemed worth while without showing the accomplishments off. Hence, as Miss Myra Belle learned to read and write fluently, it was necessary for her to prove her cultivation by speaking pieces, the florid declamations of the old south's romantic sentimentality, spoken flamboyantly and on the most public occasions possible. When she learned to play on her mother's celebrated piano, the community and the hotel patrons must be reminded of her talent by frequent volunteer performances which could be arranged almost without solicitation and which were marked more by fury of execution than by studied technique. When she learned to ride, which she did early and well, and on somewhat better mounts than the average, it was not enough for her to trot decorously about the village on a young girl's proper domestic errands or to join troupes of chaperoned contemporaries for occasional modest canters about the countryside. She must flaunt regional social prominence in spectacular riding habits and feats of break-neck audacity. As she formed her manners otherwise than on the local etiquette codes, she instinctively selected for patterns the haughty, high-tempered, emotionally reckless heroines in novels of the school of Mr. William Gilmore Simms.

But a lady's education on the southwestern border included more than the humanities. However much prudish reticences and hysterical aversions might be tests of breeding in eastern salons, dignified poise in southern Missouri required that its possessor be hard to shock.

Miss Myra Belle learned early that, far from carrying stigmas of boorishness and squalor, the ability to chew and spit tobacco expertly was merely the normal badge of mature virility. She learned that a gentleman's standing in the local social register was not affected by his getting publicly and pugnaciously "plastered," but that on the contrary many of the best planters and town capitalists paid a sort of left-handed tribute to their state of splendor by occasionally doing it. Eligible young gentlemen did not, by indulging in eye-gouging contests, bowie knife duels and family blood feuds, become fit objects of disgust and the reforming passions of women. They had merely risen to emotional emergencies in a way that was creditable to their personal honor and high spirit.

She was aware, of course, that no gentleman should address a lady profanely. On the other hand she was taught that it was not her duty to protest against the lavish stream of profane talk which constantly assailed her quickly hardened little ears on the streets, over the thin partitions of the tavern bar, or from the long summer night talk of rounders and drummers on the verandahs. Words could not hurt a young woman of almost spectacular social position. Indeed, these particular words might almost be worth learning and treasuring up for some emergency that called for the last bit of fire in a modishly volcanic temperament. Finally she learned that no true lady ever asked or cherished embarrassing suspicions about certain hard-faced and secretive but lavishly spending stock men who appeared now and then with herds of half wild cattle and horses for sale,—riding in from the southwest, down Indian Territory way.

With it all, she grew up a hotel child. That meant that there was always an audience. Lonely, child-loving strangers flattered her accomplishments beyond their worth, benevolently befuddled strangers were usually on hand to encourage her extravagances with little gifts and requests for more declamations and concerts. Teasing strangers would goad her rather ill-controlled emotional nature into tantrums one moment and spoil her the next, not caring which so long as the time was passed.

At fifteen she must have been a little more vain, a little more self-centered, a little more headstrong, officious and theatrical than in so very young a "lady" anywhere else than on the southwestern frontier would have been quite pleasant. But also considerably more resourceful and self-reliant than the average. The hotel, the frontier, an education chiefly concerned with the importance of being noticed, had taught her to take life by the horns.

The time was coming when she could put such a sophistication to use. Just when the education for ostentatious gentility was finished, in the spring of her fifteenth birthday, came the Civil War.

To southern Missouri the struggle was not so much a volcanic national emergency as an open season for neighborhood malice. Forty-year-old personal feuds between slavery and free soil sympathizers now boiled over agreeably into a stage of permissible homicide. Old family hatreds hitherto devoid of political bias drove the antagonists into the opposing armies, almost regardless of their secession opinions, for the sake of the new license to murder and despoil at sight. Toughs, bullies and congenital vagabonds whose passions for arson, murder and burglary had thus far been somewhat restrained by the peace officers, now joined volunteer outfits which quickly became irregulars; irregulars which quickly degenerated into bushwhackers and land pirates. The marches and occasional minor battles of the regular forces brought, by comparison, almost an air of tranquillity. Assassination, plunder and wanton destruction reigned again when they left.

A "lady" trained by Arkansas border standards was scarcely prepared to be horrified. The atmosphere of hatred appealed to Myra Belle's

cultivated taste for the violent emotions. The
opportunity to parade the countryside as a
dashing Confederate virago appealed to her
sense of flamboyance. Somewhere in the genteel blood of the Shirleys there was more than a
dash of Cherokee, but pity could hardly have
been a controlling emotion in any case. If a
Yankee civilian was murdered now and then by
southern night-riders, his barns burned and his
household goods plundered from the widow and
orphans, what of it? Yankee soldiers away off
somewhere in Virginia might deserve the
dignity of being killed only in honest battle,
but when these nigger-lovers came into a southern state with their notions of stealing the slaves
away from their rightful owners by some aboli-
tion outrage, this was what they should expect.

Close to the Arkansas line a sharp-faced,
beady-eyed young man named Quantrill was
organizing a band said to be responsible for most
of these vengeances. Well, the Yankees deserved it. According to the stories Myra Belle
and all other confederates heard, they had begun it first. Had not quite a few secessionists
been shot down by night-riders and had their
barns burned and their houses plundered, if you
happened to notice it? Besides, her brother

Ed Shirley himself was off in the swamps with Quantrill. No more than in his 'teens, he was already a captain. If Myra Belle could find a way to help Mr. Quantrill's outfit, you could bet your last dollar of Jeff Davis's money she would.

The way was found early and rather easily. The Quantrill gang needed, above all other things, information,—information about what the Yankee regiments were doing and planning, and where the Yankee home guard companies were, or were not; information about the mobilization of grain, fodder, horses and mules for shipment to the Yankee armies; tips on Yankee farmers and small-town personages who might have a little silver service or a little hard money in the family sock that would be good for "the cause,"—which was to say, young Mr. Quantrill's commissary and paymaster's departments. A pertly attractive young miss, already something of a privileged character in public places, who knew everybody within a hundred and fifty miles of Carthage who had ever been her father's hotel guest, could, by using her quick ears, her shrewd wit and her horsemanship incessantly, conduct a highly successful tip service. And Miss Myra Belle did.

Twenty-five, fifty and even more miles away, school girl friends and old family intimates of the Shirleys grew accustomed to seeing the dashing little creature in her feathered sombrero and bright colored riding habits gallop up to their doors on her lathered horse for overnight visits, sometimes week-long and fortnight visits. In a country of much generous and casual hospitality there was nothing particularly remarkable about this, except that Myra Belle came unescorted and unchaperoned. But this was like Myra Belle and, with the war on, the men away and the older women correspondingly busy at home, it was probably inevitable. Some of her hosts, no doubt, were in on the secret. But even when they happened to be Yankee sympathizers they merely reflected, as their guest sat chattering with girlish enthusiasm about neighborhood gossip, parties, young people's courtships and not about the war at all, that the little Shirley girl must be a good deal less of a "spitfire" and more of a lady than her reputation suggested. And when she would start home again, her sturdy insistence that she needed no escort would simply remind them that here was an exceptionally independent and resourceful youngster inclined to be pleasantly considerate of people who had a lot of work to do.

But a discreet distance along the way home Miss Myra Belle would usually leave the main road for some inconspicuous bridle path. And wherever the bridle path led deepest into the hill country or the backwoods, she was likely to meet a rough-looking, watchful young man on horse-back, or possibly half a dozen rough-looking, watchful young men. Then she would hold long talk with her audience and tell what her quick young ears had picked up and her shrewd judgment had pieced together from the neighborhood military gossip.

Or occasionally she would leave even bridle paths behind her, and gallop through swamps and underbrush to a place where the rough-looking young men were camped in scores or in hundreds. Then her brother, Captain Ed, would come and put his arm around her and young Mr. Quantrill would unbend his sullen dignity to pay her sexless but strangely thrilling compliments on her nerve and loyalty. Their "little scout," they called her, a euphemism for expert spying complicated occasionally with a little treachery to hosts. Nevertheless, she learned from it how to meet men man-fashion, and that the admiration of rough and desperate young men had a glamor about it which the society of chivalrous boy lieutenants in their gray Confederate uniforms sometimes lacked.

But before the first year was up the game was growing risky. The Yankees, too, had an intelligence service and, whether or not it was boorish enough to keep track of a prominent débutante's social engagements, it soon suspected something. In a neighborhood given over to rancorous gossip and treachery charges and aware that Ed Shirley was hiding out with Quantrill, things would have been suspected even without circumstantial evidence. But no sane heads on the Union side cared to inflame public sentiment by treating a popular young girl unchivalrously. In southern Missouri the Civil War was as much an exercise in propaganda as in bushwhacking, and a girl spy shot or even imprisoned might have affected public sentiment worse than a Confederate victory. It seems to have been decided that Myra Belle should be let off the first time with a good scare. After that all hands could settle back and meet further emergencies as they happened.

The time selected was when Ed Shirley came

home for a visit. For the Missouri war was as informal socially as it was irregular in other particulars. Men frequently left the marauding bands on both sides to get married, visit wives, do their part in family feuds, help with the farming, attend dances and keep poker engagements. The younger boys now and then even showed up for the short winter school terms. Ed was at home in the winter of 1862, quite openly and heroically, simply for a vacation.

He was there so long, in fact, that he ceased to be a family novelty and Myra Belle, early in February, rode over to the village of Newtonia, thirty-five miles away, to pick up neighborhood gossip. Quite possibly she had Captain Ed's military sophistication in mind, and certainly nothing was further from her thoughts than being interfered with. Nevertheless, one morning a Yankee cavalry squad bore down on her near the Newtonia post office and politely but efficiently arrested her.

They took her to the long, roomy, red-brick house of the town's leading citizen, Judge Ritchery, and there she found that the worst possible thing had happened. She was the prisoner of a certain Major Enos, who besides being in command of an unpleasantly large cavalry detachment, was an old neighbor who knew the local ground, the local gossip and all about the Shirleys' Confederate connections. Twice as much as any imported Yankee invader, this hideous home-town scalawag was capable of spoiling everything.

A more suave Myra Belle might have tried to get off by pleading innocence and appealing to old family friendship. But the "little scout" of the Quantrill outfit had been trained to use "scenes" rather than duplicity for getting effects. She clawed at her somewhat amused guardian, kicked him and made such violent efforts to lay on with her riding quirt that the canny major felt it advisable to throw it out the window. Then she suddenly recalled the long list of picturesque oaths with which her hotel childhood had acquainted her, and called her captor by all of them generously and sincerely. Out of breath, she could still remember that a lady's accomplishments called for something in the way of cultivated defiance. So she sat down at the Ritchery piano and forced the major to listen to an hour's concert of very loud and very Confederate music.

She gave, no doubt, a peculiarly disagreeable

morning to a man who was only trying to scare
a little spitfire without mortifying her by putting her under a guard of common soldiers. So
he is perhaps to be excused if, when he released
her, he remarked somewhat testily: "Get along
home now, Myra. And if you meet some of
my men on your way back, take a good look at
their prisoner. I'll bet you a Yankee dollar
against a rebel one that it'll be Ed."

Myra Belle ostensibly ignored the challenge.
To show her indifference she loitered in the
garden a whole quarter of an hour with Judge
Ritchery's daughter. Then, gathering a bundle
of painfully supple cherry switches—the riding
quirt had been preserved among the Federal
war trophies—she was off. The cavalry troop
on Ed Shirley's trail had almost a full half
day's start.

But the cavalry troop only knew the road-
maps and Myra Belle knew the short cuts and
the bridle paths. Whatever her horse did not
know about the efficacy of cherry switches, that
afternoon she taught him. At sunset she galloped into Carthage, appropriately dishevelled
and indignant, but an hour ahead of the Federal
cavalry.

When the troop came in with the darkness,

she was careful, as became a town heroine on the make, to receive them herself. "If you're looking for Captain Shirley," she told them with vicious irony, "you're very much too late. He had such important business up Spring River that he left a whole half an hour ago. It's too dark to follow him now, isn't it?"

The whole neighborhood heard about it, of course. The Confederates admired in their extravagant fashion and the Yankees cursed her for a dangerous vixen. At any rate, here she was, sixteen and a public celebrity. Here was a notoriety that beat speaking pieces and playing exciting gallopades on the piano for the hotel guests. Here was a fame that she could publicly flaunt and publicly relish instead of hiding as she had had to do with the little secret whispers of notice that came to her from her spying exploits.

Her whole nature had prepared her to make the most of it, but not, I think, quite agreeably. She was not going to be any emotional old Confederate's pet on account of it or even a privilegedly flirtatious heart-smasher to Mr. Quantrill's young men. Instead, she swaggered over her deed in a dour, hard-boiled little fashion and was almost as haughty and distant to those who wished to praise her for it as to pro-Yankee old maids who made up spiteful gossip about her character on the basis of her shocking language to Major Enos. But she liked it, this sensation of being both important and dangerous, better than anything else she had discovered in her whole "lady-like" education. And as the war rolled sullenly on and Mr. Quantrill's young desperadoes, now raiding in northeastern Kansas, now forced back into the Indian Territory, had less and less need of military information from southwestern Missouri, she longed to feel its thrills again and more profoundly.

When the war ended, old John Shirley, with the characteristic malevolence of old men toward altered circumstances, abandoned his inn without even bothering to find a purchaser and went to Texas. Myra Belle, as became a dutiful daughter, of course went with him, though doubtless with some annoyance at leaving a country to which Mr. Quantrill's young men were still contributing a good deal of excitement.

But her misgivings soon turned out to be largely imaginary. The Judge settled down

From "Beyond the Mississippi, 1833-'67," by Albert D. Richardson.

LAWRENCE, KANSAS
After a Quantrill Raid

From "Beyond the Mississippi, 1833-'67," by Albert D. Richardson.

A CONTEMPORARY VIEW OF SOCIAL LIFE
IN OKLAHOMA

on a farm two hours' easy trot from the rising little village of Dallas, and Dallas in 1865 was cowtown, frontier and turbulent reconstruction hamlet rolled into one. Besides, as Myra Belle before long pleasantly experienced, this north central Texas country was destined for a more neighborly relationship with southern Missouri than geography might have suggested.

For instance, when one of Mr. Quantrill's young men got into trouble with the authorities by assuming that the war was still on or that well-to-do Yankees still required something in the way of highway robbery or plunder raids to punish them for their victory, the most natural thing in the world for him to do was to hide out in the wilds of Indian territory until the excitement was over and then sociably ride over into north Texas for a well-earned vacation. So far as sheriff's warrants and requisitions were concerned, the region was almost as much No Man's Land as the territory. And it had the further advantage of containing far larger numbers of sympathizing and endlessly hospitable Confederate households. Belle doubtless helped entertain a number of such excursion parties and basked pleasantly in the admiration of rough young men who were delighted to be esteemed still as Mr. Quantrill's prowling panthers and had never, for their better reputation as serious hellions, heard of shell shock. Then in 1866 one of the parties brought along Jim Reed.

She had known him before as a Quantrill man and one of Ed's fellow fighters, though apparently almost impersonally. But in Texas Jim found a way to impress her. Was it to admire her small frontier town cultivation, flatter her hard little pride of dangerous achievement, or remind her of their mutual home-sickness? Probably he sounded all three notes with more than the average bush-whacker's energy and subtlety, for Jim's crudeness, sharpened by the war and outlawry, could hardly have appealed to her town-bred tastes for luxuries like piano-playing and elaborate manners. Yet within twenty-four hours, this young woman of hard-riding exploits and quick decisions had made up her mind to marry him.

Much to their annoyance, Judge Shirley objected. He had plenty of sympathy for the boys who were ostracised, held out of jobs and chased over the hills by Missouri's triumphant Yankees, and he did not blame them in the least for disturbing the peace of the commonwealth to get a little proper vengeance. He was glad to welcome them to Texas where the carpet-baggers confined themselves to taking the offices and did not try to set the tone for society and monopolize the business openings besides. But marrying Belle off to a fugitive from justice, no matter what justice,—for the first gentle-man of Carthage, the idea was preposterous. No daughter of his was going to take a husband who might have to go to the penitentiary even if he didn't deserve it.

While the Judge stormed in the conventional manner of southern fathers, Belle and Jim calmly rode off for an all-day picnic with Jim's excursion party and got married by a member of the outfit who boasted a justice's of peace license.

The traditions which follow are so compli-cated that authentic account of the romance is almost untraceable. Jim appears to have found it necessary to decamp for the safe seclusion of Indian Territory within a day or two after the ceremony, possibly because the Judge's protec-tive hospitality had been withdrawn. But within four months his Missouri difficulties had cleared up and he abducted the bride, with her hearty co-operation, to his home at Rich Hill.

The unreconciled Judge countered promptly by abducting her again to Texas, appealing to her diligently trained sense of decorum with the old-fashioned notion that a young southern girl always obeys her father.   Hence Jim had to make still another trip to Texas and steal her away from the paternal ranch, this time in a shower of bird-shot.   It was considerably more than a year after the marriage before the Reed household was permanently assembled.

In any case Belle found herself equipped with a husband well adapted to fortifying a strictly lady-like education with dashes of Quantrill technique.   Jim engaged in enough escapades in Missouri to keep him a large part of the time in Indian Territory, and Belle discovered the prime diversions of matrimony to be visiting him in his hide-outs.   Then in 1870 even the territory became perilous.   A rival group of nominally demobilized bushwhackers, the Shannon boys, on the trail of a feudist enemy named Fisher, made the mistake of killing Jim's brother, Scott Reed.   Jim refused to accept explanations of technical error and killed at least one Shannon out of vengeance. With an Indian Territory murder warrant out for him and unfortunately forty years too early to sell his outlaw's celebrity in Hollywood, he fled to Los Angeles.

Belle went along with her year-old daughter and when they returned as far as Texas in 1872 Judge Shirley had also a year-old grandson. Whether this circumstance reconciled him to a difficult son-in-law or whether he simply determined to make the best of things, he helped Belle acquire a ranch nine miles from the Shirley place and the group settled down to unbroken amity. Jim, to be sure, hid out in the prairies of northern Texas to be safer from old warrants and also, it seems, to facilitate certain profitable trading operations in horses of doubtful title. Whenever the notoriety of this business made Texas dangerous, he retreated to a new hiding place in Indian Territory eighty miles west of Fort Smith and famous already for nearly a generation as the hangout of Ellis Starr, the bad man of the Cherokees.

Old Ellis himself was dead, after having forced from the rest of the Cherokee nation in 1866 a formal diplomatic treaty of peace for the consideration of a good slice of the tribal wealth. But his son Tom still kept up the family associations and ex-Quantrill operators, new outlaws of the reconstruction disorder and miscellaneous young men taking discreet vacations from the activities of the new gangs of the James boys and Cole Younger, found the place a congenial health resort.

As a frequent visitor from her Texas properties, Belle found there agreeable opportunities to enlarge both her acquaintance and her sophistication. Even the social diversions on the place were instructive. Besides riding to dances after the informal Cherokee Strip custom with Jim in front of her and the handsome young half-breed boy, Tom Starr's son Sam, holding on to her by the midriff from behind, she advanced to first name intimacy with the Jameses and the Youngers.

But the real business of the establishment was far from pastoral. One night in 1873 a group of Starr retainers came down on the dugout of Watt Grayson, a Creek Indian suspected of having helped himself to the tribal funds generously, stretched his neck to a rope seven times and his wife's neck three times until they gave up $30,000.00. Belle was innocently asleep in the ranch near Dallas, but Jim was recognized. His chronic need of concealment was excitingly redoubled.

Belle, however, was equal to the emergency.

She found him hiding places in some of the best Dallas family residences, innocent-appearing jobs at near-by ranches too respectable for sheriffs to question, remote retreats in the woods and between the prairie swales when pursuit became serious. Partly, no doubt, to establish a social center that would also be helpful as an intelligence service, she started a livery stable. Soon Texas society's regard for Jim had been so far restored by her seductive patronage that he could operate almost openly again as a good family provider. The small assortment of farm nags with which she had begun business was replaced by spirited caballadas of newly broken range ponies for which no authentic bills of sale were in evidence. Visitors from up Indian Territory way sometimes eyed them with a suspicious air of recognition, but on the other hand at the Belle Reed Livery patrons from up Indian Territory way were discouraged. For the rest, Texans were disposed to be sympathetic with a gallant ex-Confederate soldier who merely helped himself from time to time to horses which a race of inferior savages were not likely to miss anyway. And Belle, without admitting anything, saw to it that Jim got his full share of this approval.

She was cultivating now the community's influential side and found the livery stable an effective point of vantage. The rich stockmen and cattle barons of the region came there to hire rigs for their town festivities, the lawyers and politicians of the thriving county seat found the service snappy and her nags the most reliable for their errands in the country. The proprietress's technique was a model combination of social charm, business-like friendliness and perfect circumspection. Poor little thing, they pitied her. The carpet-baggers had made her husband a fugitive, yet here she was with grit enough to stand up for him and sense enough to run a first-class livery stable,—and a lady, besides.

Their reconstruction passions boiled over in chivalrous admiration. They would see that their wives did something about this, and they did. Belle began to receive calls and be invited to receptions and suppers. She gave recitations again to delighted audiences and played the melancholy popular airs of the period on fortunate hostesses' pianos. With just enough reserve amid the gayeties to impress the audience with her heroic firmness under peculiar afflictions, she gained a sympathy which she was careful not to alienate by encouraging philanderers. Even in Dallas's circle of ante-bellum dowagers it became a moderate social distinction to know the little livery stable keeper intimately.

It paid, and paid more and more in the profits of Jim's open-air stud. From an ardently hunted fugitive he gradually became able to cheer a devoted family by appearing often and with only the slightest precautions. Even when one of the strings of horses offered for sale happened by some geographical negligence to be taken on the Texas side, Belle's cultivation of a great lady's social estate proved positively strategic.

Jim was arrested, of course, but a town swarming with the gritty little wife's protectors and defenders saw to it that other embarrassing matters in his record were not pressed. But his release did not occur soon enough to satisfy a highborn lady's mettlesome impatience. Meeting a deputy sheriff by the name of Nichols on the street, Belle remonstrated with him about this and informed him in her best Quantrill border war accents that if her husband was not turned loose at once, she would attend to Nichols' killing personally.

A few days later Nichols actually was shot dead on the public street. With the acute gifts for inattention characteristic of a cowtown crowd in such embarrassments, none of the numerous spectators could remember just who shot him. But, in public repute at least, Belle got credit for the first notch on her gun.

In any case, her protective edifice held firm. Whether she actually shot Nichols or even prompted the assassination, are questions that are still debated by all but the most lurid-minded experts. The one certain thing about it is that the passing of Mr. Nichols enhanced her reputation as a lady of violence and that nothing was done about it.

Quite evidently, from the local viewpoint, a young woman who fortified a desire to kill a carpet-bagger's deputy with social standing, the modish accomplishments and a record of scouting for Quantrill, might consider herself privileged. Not only that, but the privilege extended to all the family. Jim was almost immediately released.

But the popular young husband's career as a professional reconstruction misfit was nearly over. Federal rewards for his capture dead or alive might not appeal to members of his wife's social circle in Dallas but they rendered his potential carcass highly attractive to casual strangers who happened to be immune to Confederate traditions. In the summer of 1875 he was returning from a congenial stay at Mrs. Reed's livery stable to the scene of his Territory border operations. A plausible travelling companion by the name of Morris advised him not to offend an eccentric old farmer near McKinney, Texas, by going to dinner in his house with a loaded Winchester.

The confiding Mr. Reed left the weapon outside. Almost immediately Mr. Morris, on the chivalrous ruse of pretending to fetch water from the pump for his hostess, walked to the horse corral and procured his. Then, entering the room strategically from the rear, he filled the valuable Mr. Reed full of fatal lead.

But Mr. Morris's reckonings failed to take account of the self-control and tactful malevolence of a lady whose training had been chiefly in vindictive pride. In order to claim the reward for Jim's body, it was necessary to have it identified, and in a Texas summer, it was necessary to make the identification quickly or not at all. Lacking a wide personal acquaintance in the neighborhood and knowing only its disposition to shield Jim under all circumstances, the pleasant strategy occurred to him of sending for Belle and wringing the identification out of her grief.

Belle came and looked at what was left of Jim dry-eyed and casually, but at Mr. Morris scornfully and for an uncomfortably long while.

"Mr. Morris," she said with her best Dallas evening party irony, "I am very sorry, but you've killed the wrong man. If you want the reward for Jim Reed's body, you will have to kill Jim Reed."

She had learned more than how to stock a livery stable since she boiled over in the Ritchery parlor and cursed Major Enos.

By logical irony it was her widowhood from an outlaw which released her for a career of outlawry on her own account. Hitherto she had needed to emphasize her own respectability in order to give a certain countenance to Jim's operations. By holding herself up as nothing more dangerous than an extraordinarily dashing frontier belle, capricious, hot-tempered but essentially moral and conventional, she had managed to make her husband's rather appalling record seem to her region like a list of semi-patriotic peccadilloes. Her own part in his escapades had the air of dare-deviltry, no doubt, but it was of the praiseworthy, romantic sort rather than the woman desperado's. The technique by which she had become privileged also paid in other considerations. Like many of the border bandits driven into outlawry by the reconstruction disorders, Jim appears to have been a devoted husband. So long as Belle's popularity could keep him free for his operations, he was a good provider of luxuries as well as of livery stock.

With Jim gone, her chief motive for discretion was removed, and at the same time she required what only shady activities could procure. Her father was dead and her mother's affairs were tangled. She had two young children to rear, her taste for luxuries in horses and music—some say books also—to keep up and, at the moment, a relatively expensive social position to support. The only ways she knew of meeting these obligations were Jim's ways.

For a time she seems to have done no more than conduct through her livery stable a sort of tip service for Jim's old associates in border depredations. She moped a good deal about

Jim's death and wrote letters, full of complaints about such lady-like ailments as headache and nervousness, to his brother in Missouri urging him to come down to Texas and take proper vengeance. With her own career as a hotel parlor entertainer to encourage her, she had hopes of making a child dancer of her little girl, Pearl, on the Dallas stage. But after a few performances the over-stimulated infant fainted, a prey to some nervous disorder, and returned to the nursery. Belle was back again on her own resources.

If she must scandalize, then, she would incur the penalties with ostentatious defiance.

She began deserting the livery stable for days at a time and taking madcap horse-back rides out into the prairies. Dallas, once so indulgent when such journeys were known to take her to rendezvous with her husband, now frowned and gossiped that she was meeting with bands of horse-stealing outlaws. When she let the livery stable virtually drift out of her ownership and still came back from these expeditions well provided with money, the tale went around that she was sharing the outlaws' proceeds. From a general favorite she became first suspect and then an object of sinister avoidance. Standing up for Jim had been wifely and proper, but these outlaws were rustling Texas horses and cattle and the situation was serious. Was she getting a share of their spoils for conducting an information service, for helping them on their raids—or for something worse?

By 1877 the town had a nubbin of delectably pornographic gossip to confirm it in the worst. Out on an all-day gallop Belle and a young girl of harum-scarum reputation named Emma Jones were caught by a Texas norther near a cross roads settlement. They took shelter in the lee of the village store and when noon came built a fire to warm their coffee, using the rear wall of the building as a back log. The coffee was successful but the store was reduced to ashes. Belle next day found herself in the Dallas jail on charges of arson and malicious mischief.

At her first hearing, however, the dignity and refinement of her bearing completely ravished an elderly stockman named Patterson from the remoter ranges. Stirred to the depths of Freudian generosity, the amiable dotard sought her out and inquired how much it would cost to pay her legal expenses and get the charges dismissed. Belle, without batting an eye or making a promise, told him that by the most conservative estimates it would cost $2,500.00. The philanthropic Patterson promptly sold cows and delivered the wad in cash. A day or two later the arson charge was withdrawn, as had been all along a foregone conclusion, and Mrs. Reed released on payment of a nominal fine for malicious mischief, approximately $2,490.00 to the good.

Mr. Patterson enjoyed her company at one or two innocuous hotel dinners and was put off in his collection efforts with a plea of stupendous legal expenses. Then he sought advice from friends and was of course urged to file fraud charges and prosecute. But here, one regrets to say, his very excess of doting chivalry led him to blast a lady's reputation.

"Hell, leave her keep it," was his epigram. "I reckon after what she's had to put up with, she's earned every cent of it."

Dallas promptly assumed with snickers and some indignation that what the widow had "put up with" referred to the uncomely but notoriously amorous Patterson's advances, and cheerfully condemned its former parlor heroine to the ostracism of loose women. Belle had finished with relying on caste to countenance indiscretions.

Yet she took the blow with characteristic social strategy, seeming by her dour haughtiness to snub Dallas before it could snub her. With the help of Mr. Patterson's contribution she blossomed out in new thoroughbreds, new and more modish riding habits, so that strangers in the town often fancied her to be some eccentric Kentucky or Virginia heiress feeling herself too superior to the normal run of Texans to exchange the common courtesies. But she was also using the Patterson money to send her little son to the Reed mother-in-law's in Missouri and Pearl, the retired danseuse, to a friend's in Arkansas; and she paid for their board and schooling for two years in advance. Yet in all this she was merely getting ready to prove to Dallas' horrified satisfaction that to call a lady harsh names is a sure way to make her dangerous.

In 1878 she was arrested for horse-stealing. She was getting too bold to stop with acting as fence and tipster for the outlaws and had begun preying on the neighbors themselves. But she was also by now far too contemptuous of the conventions which had ostracised her to

submit to being tried for it.   In jail she turned
the wiles of a distressed and persecuted gentle-
woman upon an emotional turnkey.   A week
later, in the dead of a glamorous spring night,
she had eloped with him.

In a month he was back again in the somewhat unsympathetic bosom of his family, a
sadder turnkey and a much wiser one about
erotic infatuations.   His story is plausible if
only because it is so amusingly consistent with
the widow Reed's temperament.   For the har-
assed philanderer insisted that his part in the
escapade was not that of a lover but of escort,
cook, horse-wrangler, wood-fetcher and water-
carrier, at the point of his own pistol.   It was
he who had escaped from an unpleasant and
humiliating imprisonment rather more than
Belle.

Nevertheless, Mrs. Reed was through with
Dallas jail bars and the snubs of Dallas society.   She was out in the wilds for good.

That year and the next she rode the ranges
of northwest Texas, the Oklahoma and Texas
Panhandles with as thoroughgoing a group of
desperadoes and cut-throats as ever missed a
deserved national celebrity.   Jim French, the

Blue Duck and Jack Spaniard were their leaders but fugitives from border justice, highwaymen whose gangs had been decimated by prison sentences, temperamental half-breeds from the reservations, dangerously Americanized Mexicans from New Mexico and cowboys gone wrong through rustling often swelled their numbers to nearly fifty. They picked up mavericks in the Atascosa territory, rustled stampeded cattle from the trail drivers on their way to the Kansas shipping points, plied Jim Reed's old specialty of stealing horses from the Indians, held up cow-town banks occasionally and did a little road agentry on the stage routes. In general they lived by villainy and, so far as the circumstances of the frontier would permit, lived well. They seem to have maintained some contact, or at least an hospitable acquaintance, with what was left of the Younger and Sam Bass gangs of train robbers.

Belle's own activities with such a remote and secretive troupe are necessarily somewhat apocryphal. She dominated them a good deal by the force of her will and her proud, increasingly harsh personality. Her reserve made the boisterous keep their distance and if any of the gang enjoyed her favors, it was by her wish, not theirs. Her commanding airs and her great lady's pose made them rustle to do the hard work of the camp for her so that when she did her share occasionally and with a certain suffering ostentation, she gained credit for immense condescensions. Her shrewdness and her astonishing literacy got her standing, if not as a leader of active operations, at least as the outfit's brains.

She knew, too, how to use her sophistication with frontier harshness sparingly enough to make it effective. Weeks would go by without her indulgence in a word or action unworthy of the first lady of Carthage. But when her hat blew off on a cross country gallop with the Blue Duck and that scorner of empty mannerisms failed to repair the mishap, he found himself looking down the widow Reed's revolver. "Now, damn your greasy hide," she threatened him. "You pick up that hat, and let this be a lesson in how to treat a lady that you won't forget!" By the gang's traditions, the Blue Duck never failed in courtesy afterward.

He had reason not to, for Belle shortly paid him more than handsomely for his condescen-

From "Hell on the Border," by S. W. Harman.

BELLE STARR AND THE BLUE DUCK
A Boy and Girl Friendship of the Great Open Spaces

sion. The Blue Duck, on one of their Indian Territory expeditions, borrowed $2,000.00 from the outfit's temporarily flush treasury and lost it in a poker game at Fort Dodge. Belle sympathized with his suspicion that such an expert could not have been deprived of a fortune honestly. Next day, with a gun in each hand, she strolled into the gambling house and raided the pot for $7,000.00. "There's a little change due one of my friends, gentlemen," she informed them with a flash of her most charming irony. "If you want it back, come down to the territory and get it."

To this period, too, belongs the legend of her descent on a prosperous cow country seat in the character of a genteel southern widow seeking investment opportunities. She charmed all with her accomplishments and cultivated manners. At the end of the week she had removed from the hotel and taken up her quarters as the guest of the banker's wife.

Then one afternoon the banker himself, sitting in his office in conference with her on the business outlook, was alarmed to observe that he was covered by her pistol. Still covered, he obligingly unlocked the safe, handed over its contents and submitted to binding and gagging. Mrs. Reed rode off into the safe prairie darkness. By next morning, when the banker returned to his home and was still trying to convince a suspicious wife that it was after all not so bad as an elopement, the assets were safe in the gang's treasury.

But the law, having settled with Sam Bass and the James family, was ready to close in on the Blue Duck and Jack Spaniard. With her usual shrewdness, Belle saw the portents and retired for a vacation to her late husband's recreation ground at the Starr ranch in the Cherokee country. Even here danger threatened, or perhaps the charming Sam Starr opened her eyes to the pleasing opportunities for rustling near the thriving new cow town of Ogallala, Nebraska. Here they went early in 1880. When they came back a year and a half later, urged, it is said, by neighborhood suspicions that their herds were increasing by more means than breeding and purchase, they were married.

In a remote spot on the Canadian river, eight miles from the postoffice of Eufaula, the Starrs located a thousand-acre claim and settled down to a life of what, for the Indian

country, passed as social leadership. They
brought Pearl there with her exciting vestiges
of stage child's coquetry. The hostess, prospering from her years with the Blue Duck in
Nebraska, ordered sumptuous wardrobes from
the St. Louis department stores. From somewhere, too, she acquired the last symbol of
frontier cultivation, a piano.

The cabin was plain, with puncheon floor
and calico print nailed over its log partitions
for wall paper. Buffalo horns and deer antlers
did duty for its interior decorations, instead of
old masters, more creditably still, instead of
Indian Territory store chromos. But chance
visitors, always easily impressed in the '80s,
marveled at the tastily chosen bric-a-brac on
the rustic mantel. And if we are to believe a
lady's most plausible biographer, the intellectual tastes of John Shirley, the first gentleman
of Carthage, were represented by rows of
books "of a sort as are seen in the best
libraries."

Now and then, the chatelaine left her half-
breed husband and her rustically charming
daughter to visit, it was represented, the popular eastern watering places; likewise, as the
biographer puts it, to "spend money lavishly

and mingle freely with the wealth and culture of the nation." Once, at White Sulphur Springs, it is insisted that her playing of doleful ante-bellum popular airs on the piano charmed a circle of old Confederate ladies from Richmond into tears.

Did she really? Or was it simply that Indian Territory admiration could not contemplate the occasional mysterious absence of such splendor without explaining it in folk lore?

The best authenticated eastern visit, however, was not to a fashionable watering place or so mysteriously overlaid with tradition. "Now, Pearl," Belle wrote to her daughter in 1883 in one of the most genteelly persuasive explanations of a sentence to a reformatory yet penned west of the Mississippi, "there is a vast difference in that place and a penitentiary; you must bear that in mind and not think of mamma being shut up in a gloomy prison.

"It is said to be one of the finest institutions in the United States, surrounded by beautiful grounds, with fountains and everything nice. There I can have my education renewed, and I stand greatly in need of it. Sam will have to attend school and I think it will be the best thing that ever happened for him. And now you must not be unhappy and brood over our absence. It won't take the time long to glide by and as we come home we will get you, and then we will have such a nice time."

The institution thus eulogized was the Detroit House of Correction. Belle and Sam were sentenced to it, as often ironically happens to famous desperadoes, for a mere peccadillo. The heroine of bank raids, rustling by the herd and at least one possible killing of a sheriff, fell before the federal courts at last for stealing a lone colt.

It was not, they insisted, even their theft. A plotting enemy, a former federal marshal, had publicly advised them to steal it, so their alibi ran, to avenge themselves on a neighbor who had killed their best stallion. Then, having shrewdly pointed suspicion, the wretch stole it himself and only turned the animal loose in the Starr pasture when his own guilt was about to come out. The court, however, either held that possession of a stolen article was nine points of a conviction, or that the Starrs deserved some punishment for their reputation. They went north with the spring batch of prisoners.

Belle took the blow with her usual nobleness. She was pale and gently proud with the court, haughtily contemptuous of newspaper reporters. At the House of Correction her dignified pathos was all but ravishing.

The warden, preparing to instruct her in her duties in the prison factory, invited her to "Take a chair, please." His meaning was for the new inmate to pick up a chair frame and follow him into the work-room where women prisoners were putting the cane seats in place. But Belle replied with a weary sadness: "No, in this place, I think I should stand, thanks." When her social error was tactfully explained to her, she smiled tenderly and reproached herself for her thoughtlessness.

At such graceful tactics the warden melted and placed her on the lightest work available. The matron wept over the charming wardrobe from the St. Louis department stores when it was replaced by the prison uniforms, talked current literature with her charge in off hours and urged her to write a book about "the pleasant sides of work house life." Belle returned after nine months with a justifiable sense of having secured a new social triumph.

Unfortunately, she took out her expanded assurance on the luckless Pearl, now, by Territory standards, of marriageable age. With her accomplishments, distinguished ancestry and gentle breeding, Pearl, it was decided, must have nothing less than a "$25,000.00 man" and Belle adopted the methods of all aggressive dowagers in seeing to it that she got him.

A youth of otherwise eligible qualifications appeared without the required minimum and was haughtily sent packing. But he hung around the neighborhood and Belle, resorting to maternal stratagem, thoughtfully sent him a note, signed Pearl, announcing that a $25,000.00 suitor (as yet wholly fictitious) had arrived and been accepted. The spurned youth took his dismissal philosophically and departed to marry as best he could on the rebound.

But unfortunately for Cherokee Strip social advancements, the territory was given to gigantic neighborhood picnics. At one of these a year afterward the suitor appeared and was horrified to discover Pearl without the $25,000.00 husband. Explanations followed, mutual condolences, and also seduction. Belle promptly chased the guilty bridegroom out of the country with a flourish of six-shooters. By almost equally ferocious tactics she secured Pearl's consent to a marriage with an infatuated livery stable proprietor worth considerably less than $25,000.00.

But her poise was weakening. Sam's position in the criminal records grew seriously embarrassing. He had to spend most of 1885 in New Mexico dodging warrants for a post-office robbery. When he came back he was first shot up by a posse and then, after he had been arrested and his bond comfortably arranged, shot again in a quarrel over the ownership of his horse at a dance in Whitefield.

The neighborhood, too, was filling up with white settlers bringing with them the conventions which had punished her at Dallas. What with the family's disorderly notoriety and Pearl's public disgrace, her glamor was becoming every month less and less that of a wilderness social arbitress and more that of a common hell cat's. An acquittal on a horse-stealing charge in 1886, on no better alibi than she had had three years previously, was received by the neighborhood with more signs

From "Hell on the Border," by S. W. Harman.

BELLE AND SAM STARR

On Horses Whose Ownership Was Temporarily Not Being Questioned by the Police

of annoyance than of sympathy. Even when, in the rough riding exhibitions at the Sebastian County fair in 1887, she picked up the editor of the local newspaper with a wild swoop from the saddle, the crowd which once had feared and paid homage, merely jeered.

She was getting fat, dowdy, shrewish-tempered and, worst of all, she was losing her discretion. In 1888 a sinisterly genteel person named Edgar Watson came in vaguely from the southeast with his wife to become the Starrs' tenant. In womanly confidences, Belle wormed it out of the woman that Watson was wanted on a murder charge in Florida.

In the days of her skill at man management the mere possession of this secret would have enabled her to attach Watson to her enterprises as long as she had use of him. She used it now merely to inflame a silly quarrel. Watson took a letter for her at the Eufaula postoffice and forgot to deliver it. When it turned up a few weeks later she refused his explanations and treated him as a wilful mail robber. His natural retort was to taunt her with Sam's still-pending embarrassment over the post-office burglary.

"I don't suppose the federal officers would

trouble you," she crushed him, "but the Florida officers might."

For the terrorized Mr. Watson the threat was too much. Alone, so that no effective witnesses could be summoned against him, he ambushed her near his house while she was returning from the trial of one of Sam's cousins for the family vice—horse stealing. He knocked her off her saddle with a charge of turkey-shot. When she was safely on the ground, unconscious, he removed her own weapons and shot her again in the neck and breast until she died.

It was on her forty-third birthday. But one suspects that she had already learned all that she cared to know of what a woman may get by taking life with the high hand.

THE EXTINCTION OF A COMET

CALIFORNIA was still greeting women with huzzahs. Five men to the woman, the rowdy population of its principal seaport starved erotically in the grim hilarities of a kind of community club life. Ten and twenty to one the proportion ran in the permanent mining towns; a hundred to one, or a hundred to none at all, in the remote outposts.

Miners sweating feverishly for wealth would declare a whole day's holiday to install the first bride, the first waitress, or possibly the first traveling adventuress, in her new home with proper ceremony. Or they would loiter for hours about the covered wagon camps of new arrivals from the seacoast or overland, waiting to stare at the travel-worn and perhaps none too comely pioneer women with the tireless curiosity of children inspecting an organ-grinder's monkey.

In San Francisco the passage of a good-looking, well-dressed young woman down the street was the signal for a breathless silence and the distraction of all glances from whatever had been the business in hand. Two years before she would certainly have been followed, not by impudent mashers or obscurely fascinated degenerates, but by a knot of young men uncontrollably allured but naïvely respectful. That, to be sure, by 1853, was already passing. One man in six, now, had either a wife or definite prospects of one. The others at least had more women of the sort who could be shared in common, or passed from one to another with the convenient legal formalities of what seventy years later was to be called "progressive polygamy." But the air was still tense with frustrations too deep for frankness of speech or the release of action, frustrations which for years placed women upon pinnacles of glamor, awe and seductive attraction which no American women had attained before and few women anywhere had attained except when small towns received victorious armies.

Haughty beauties felt their pride stirred to new strategies of malevolence. The capricious redoubled their caprices, the frivolous their frivolities. Neurotic women felt themselves challenged, according to the form their neurosis took, to a more ardent wantonness or to new and more spiteful pruderies. By whatever point in posture, intonation or social technique the individual woman normally most expressed her sex, there, with the early California women, was sex most exaggerated. Men of the predestined head-of-the-family type, themselves noted for exceptional attractions to women, delayed for years in bringing out wives and fiancées to breathe the demoralized air of incitement and amorous veneration, delayed until neglect passed into separation, and separation, in some of the least credible cases, into positive desertion. Yet many who took the risk lived to regret it, as unsettled wives, deceitful wives, hysterically flirtatious, runaway, adulterous and brazenly promiscuous wives contributed their quota of gaudy scandal to California's early domestic annals.

A city, a state, a sudden and dramatically realized new era stalked about boiling with vitality and in the grip of an all but intolerable sex fixation. Yet men, except in warfare, characteristically find the means to make such emotional surcharges endurable. Greek Argonauts would doubtless have met the emergency by inventing new legends and redoubling the orgiastic ardors of their devotions to Aphrodite. Their American namesakes, hav-

ing cultivated the Puritan reticences in place
of superstition, and jocosity instead of an
esthetic imagination, kept the tension below
the hysteria line by outlawing it from serious
mention. It could be referred to, the code
permitted, under definitely ribald circumstances, but only with slapstick humor and
loud guffaws.

How would a community, thus stretched on
racks of frustration, receive, not Aphrodite
Pandemus, but a world-renowned adventuress?
How would a woman who lived by charm,
caprice and physical glamor, and hitherto had
lived prosperously and famously, react to the
tension? California was soon to know.

The semaphore flashed on Telegraph Hill
on the 21st of May. The *Northerner* was in
from the Isthmus. Pouring down for mail,
news, family reunions and the satisfaction of
endless curiosities about nothing in particular,
the crowd found that Senator Gwin and Congressman Weller were there with the condescending familiarities of politicians and pompous Washington gossip. But it also found
Lola Montez.

"Everybody is in a fever to catch a glimpse
of the lioness," wrote the *San Francisco*

Herald somewhat hectically. "Whether she comes as danseuse, authoress, politician, beauty, blue-stocking or noble lady . . . she will be seen, admired, sung, courted, gone mad over here as elsewhere."

Such compliments, indeed, had more factors behind them than a sex tension and the mercurial temperament of the forty-niners. Lola's prominence, for instance, and the range of American infatuations in the 1850s.

More, if possible, even than now American imagination in the ante-bellum heyday was feverishly and pruriently inquisitive as to the doings of royalty. Kings cast a spell over us by seeming to be still mystically dangerous to our newly won liberties. They did not, as yet, consent to interviews, receive the industrial noblesse of our Main streets in chattily democratic audiences and send their sons to mingle tactfully with the crowds at our polo tournaments. They were still grandly aloof, fascinating us with the luster of the diabolic, the mysterious and the unattainably elevated all at once. Lola had been not a King, of course. But almost more glamorous to the love-starved Californians, she had been a royal mistress.

Moreover, only a little less than kings and for similar reasons, the titled nobility dazzled us. And majesty in Bavaria had created Lola Montez Countess of Landsfeldt. True, this was in 1847 and since 1848 the Bavarian court had done all in its power to quiet the title through edicts of repeal and exile. But to American curiosity, and western curiosity especially, any patent of nobility, however new, however gained and however long abated, was sufficiently authentic.

Along with its morbid interest in rank, the country maintained an almost hysterical passion for revolutionaries. It was less disillusioned than to-day by experience; it still accepted as gospel the view that its institutions were the perfect goal of all human political progress. It still cherished evangelically and literally the ideal of a world full of republican commonwealths operating under constitutions and social arrangements built as literally as possible from the American model. So when any European idealist or demagogue struck a blow at royal prerogatives or aristocratic privileges, American opinion conceived that he had paid us the perfect compliment of imitation and automatically elevated him, along with

LOLA MONTEZ
After Steiler

Greek bandits, plausible South American dictators, Irish bog-fighters and Hungarian publicity geniuses, to the numerous and somewhat confusing galaxy of its momentary heroes.

Now Lola hit us on both our blind sides by being at once royal and revolutionary. What is more, in one stroke of daring and diligently exploited idealism she had lost both her king and her revolution.

Thus in an age of shameless sentimentality she came to California ideally equipped for an emotional conquest with the doubly melancholy glamor of a lost cause and a broken heart.

Finally, the lioness was also a European stage celebrity. The nation which in the past decade had paid its tribute of worshipping admiration to Jenny Lind and Fanny Ellsler was still bent on proving to the world that it knew how to show a European stage celebrity the appreciation that was due her. All the more because the backwoods republic was suspect of a lack of authentic taste in the arts would her reception be gorgeous, frenetic and, when necessary to make our esthetic raptures apparent to doubters, a trifle injudicious. As for California, it had an exceptional stake in this cultural ostentation since Jenny Lind and Fanny Ellsler had not visited there at all.

To be sure, not much of the countess' celebrity quite stood up biographically. She was certainly not Spanish and there were competent critics unkind enough to say she was no dancer. The daughter of an Irish subaltern's runaway marriage with a music hall entertainer—some say laundress—she herself had eloped at nineteen with an Indian army captain, to be divorced five years later for scandalous misconduct. London society had given even her dancing a cold shoulder because in the divorcee the misconduct had doubled its pace and its publicity,—and possibly its profits. Moreover, the divorce decree had not been final; and later when she trapped a wealthy but not too intelligent young Life Guard subaltern, she had had to leave England to escape prosecution for bigamy.

She had mingled with royalty, certainly. But sophisticated Europe had jeered, rather than admired, her way of doing it. Once in Berlin her runaway horse had tactfully carried her straight into the personal bodyguard of the visiting Czar Nicholas I of all the Russias, and the cuts with a riding quirt which she had given a protesting Uhlan had amused the Romanoff sense of humor. Nicholas had afterward shown her some attentions and possibly helped her out of an embarrassing intrigue with some of the Polish revolutionaries in Warsaw. But much of this was taken, even by revolutionists themselves, to prove that the Romanoffs lacked breeding.

Her affair with Ludwig of Bavaria had been sheer comedy, marred by bad judgment and worse manners. It was, of course, in the nature of royal institutions that she had cast a spell over a sixty-year-old sovereign, a sentimental dotard who wrote feeble love poetry and pried incessantly into the affairs of private citizens. It was amusing that she should worm out of him a title, a pension and a gingerbread palace in Munich. But she had used her position, as no self-respecting royal mistress would have done, to humiliate the queen. She had swaggered through the streets of Munich, lashing gendarmes with her riding whip, swearing at tradesmen, "siccing" her bull-dog on her enemies, the Jesuits. She had even denied, which was unwarrantably insolent to royalty extending its favors, that she *was* the royal mistress.

Worst of all, she had mismanaged her revolution. She had blustered and offended when what the Bavarian situation required was finesse and tactful leadership. A barbarian in culture, akin to but hardly on a par with modern Hollywood standards, she had interfered and bullied in the affairs of the country's exclusive and tradition-enamored university until she provoked the quite unnecessary rebellion which swept her from the country and Ludwig from his throne.

There was a good deal of the gutter-snipe, one fears, in Marie Dolores Eliza Gilbert-James-Heald, Countess of Landsfeldt. Albert Vandam, a member of a certain circle of Parisian wits and littérateurs, including Dumas, Beranger, Flaubert and Dujarrier of *La Presse*, had discovered, before Ludwig and California, the dangers of making too much of her. With Gallic finality he had paid his tribute that she had neither talent, manners nor address, but "only her beauty and her impudence."

But California did not know this. California in 1853 knew only her celebrity and was prepared to worship, and equally prepared to crush her with its burlesquing wit and its savage emotional tensions if the worship were not returned.

So the "royal mistress" disembarked while the crowd about Senator Gwin and Congressman Weller thinned perceptibly. It was not, perhaps, a full-blown civic ovation that she received, for Pacific communications were too slow in 1853 to prepare orgies of ticker tape, massed bands and mayor's reception committees in advance. The city never knew when a ship was coming, and seldom knew until it arrived what celebrities would be on it. So, although it had had rumors that La Montez might be along some time that spring or summer, she actually took them somewhat by surprise.

Nevertheless, an impressive crew of volunteer outriders swept about her carriage on its dusty trip up the windy streets toward the sand-hills, while a sturdier but less fortunate little procession loped, trotted or strode with magnificently Californian vigor on foot in its wake. The extent of the compliment is indicated in the fact that scores of young. men about town that day were late for the distribution of the *Northerner's* mail at the post office. They were waiting about the lobbies and under the galleries of a hotel famous in four continents for having suites said to cost fifty dollars daily, for some sort of a personal contact with eminence.

It did not come and here, one suspects, Lola misplayed her first card in the game for California popularity. The Californians were ripe to yearn but their attitude was one of insatiable curiosity rather than abasement. They were not prepared to see much use in one who would not be shaken hands with, pawed over, asked innocent questions about the court menus and the cut of the king's whiskers, and who did not reply to each sign of interest with gracious and rather lengthy speeches. They were ready to overwhelm women with an almost hysterical devotion, but they demanded that women be at least politely responsive. Their extreme sex interest and its constant inhibitions made them abnormally sensitive to slights and the woman who gave tactless indications of feeling herself better than they were was in danger of making herself the victim of their terrible burlesquing humor. The royal mistress put herself in the path of this disaster by keeping to her apartments in solitary grandeur for five days.

A woman chiefly compounded of beauty and impudence felt ecstatic admiration in the air, one suspects, and reacted to it with contemptuous superiority rather than with the winning impersonal friendliness which was all that the California bachelors asked. And there were perhaps other and even less appealing motives for haughty aloofness. When her vogue as a dancer had passed in the east, the countess had found her notoriety as a royal mistress and a revolutionist still profitable. Her manager had hit on the happy idea of exhibiting her at receptions where the curious, the social climbers and the pawers-over of museum rarities might win the honor of introductions to her at the price of a dollar a head. If the California venture ever reached this stage, the receptions might go better provided the clamorous male population of San Francisco had not been received by her prematurely and gratis.

Still, such misgivings were delicately suppressed during the days of the social quarantine. On the surface things went encouragingly. Reporters described her personal charms exuberantly, and with better accuracy than the *New York Tribune* had earlier displayed when a young journalist was so stirred by her Spanish make-up that he referred to her chestnut locks and blue Irish eyes as "Spanish black eyes and ringlets." Although something was lacking of the generosity of the Warsaw critic who years before had attributed to her twenty-six of the twenty-seven points of perfect Spanish beauty and had added the eulogy that "her finely shaped calves are the lowest rungs of a Jacob's ladder leading to heaven," yet the American plan of complimentary discourse did its utmost.

The compliments were indirect as well as personal. Lola fashions were advised by the best modistes and the best dry goods stores. At the Pioneer Race Track a gray mare named Lola Montez made her appearance and won three heats for the impressive profit of fifteen hundred dollars. The city was disposed to be generous. If the lady was slow about making friends, perhaps this was etiquette with royal mistresses; perhaps she was getting acclimated. She might be waiting for her first public appearance to expand and become approachable. Suspending judgment, the curious swarmed

down to the box office sale for her performance of Lady Teazle, paid $65.00 for the first
seat, $25.00 for the second, $5.00 for the bulk
of the orchestra while even the gallery gods
were forced to pay $1.00.

Notoriety, for the time being, triumphed.
It is probable that her Lady Teazle was wholly
bad, for even with all her assurance the royal
mistress had not dared attempt the legitimate
drama before her American tour. She lacked
voice, repose, dignity and certainly the subtle
wit necessary to play the part of a Sheridan
heroine. Yet the *San Francisco Herald*, while.
politely regretting that she was "deficient in
training," evidently sympathized with an audience which had given "unqualified tokens of
admiration." And the *Alta California* abandoned reserves altogether to insist that the
Teazle performance "evinced all that grace
and vitality which might be expected of one
who had turned the heads of princes and un-
mercifully scored editors and assailants."

But Lady Teazle was simply a feeder to
curiosity. Next night came *Yelva*, a melodrama of the Russian steppes and a part considerably more adapted to her talents since it
was extravagantly emotional and could be

played in pantomime as well. And *Yelva* itself was simply an introductory piece to her world-famous *Spider Dance*. A young Andalusian girl, in this spectacular figure, begins dancing and soon discovers the presence of a spider in her petticoats. From then on, to the excitingly Freudian concern of early Victorian audiences, the turn became a process of discovering more spiders in her skirts, shaking them out with risqué but not very revealing gymnastics, and stamping them to death with hysterical enthusiasm. Except for the slightly terrifying situation of the young Andalusian, it is somewhat difficult to gauge the appeal of such a pantomime except on the score that La Montez was exceptionally energetic and that, off the stage, in 1853 it was still the convention for charming young women, suffering from insect invasions, either to faint or to die of stings before making an effort to remove the invaders in public. But whatever the charm was, it rendered the audience ecstatic and the *Alta California* almost lyric:

"Witty, spirited, sparkling," was its tribute. "Eccentric and singular . . . a very comet of her sex; and we watch her course with the same emotions that we follow the motions of that erratic body flying through space, alone, unguided, reckless and undestined. . . . If we could know the wishes of a heart which is, we are inclined to believe, that of a noble woman, the knowledge would doubtless turn the lip that whispers busy scandal white with shame."

On May 30 she revealed the depths of her sufferings for liberty and all that California yearned to know about court intrigue and etiquette in a play called *Lola Montez in Bavaria.* Actually, the piece was a hastily assembled contraption of vaguely related tableaux, dance figures and dialogues whose main exploitation purpose may be observed in the scene headings: "Lola the Danseuse," "Lola the Politician," "Lola the Countess" and "Lola the Revolutionist and Fugitive." Incidentally, it foiled San Francisco's most intimate curiosities by representing her relations to King Ludwig as strictly inspirational and platonic, and it was followed somewhat inconsistently by a "sailor's dance and horn-pipe" in which the heroine of liberalism stepped out of character to display in pantomime "the vicissitudes of sailors' life . . . a shipwreck, the roar of the angry ocean, the howling of the storm, etc."

Nevertheless, the insistence on her nobleness

persisted. The *Herald* exulted that her "tact
. . . covered the multitude of imperfections"
even in the play itself, and referred to a "continued storm of applause." The *Alta California* felt that she had developed with the
piece's inchoate action and, in a frenzy of ad-
jectival enthusiasm, hailed her rise from "the
trifling, wayward, capricious and spoiled court
pet" to "the dignified and calm though im-
pulsive and generous woman." A little later
when *Lola Montez in Bavaria* was repeated,
the press was still able to refer to her "peculiar
earnestness of manner and utterance, her depth
of feeling and power to display the passions of
an ardent and high-souled woman."

Thus in spite of the chilling effects of her
first five days of haughtiness, San Francisco
was won. If it was won less by her merits
than by the city's determination to find her
glamor veracious, so much more did her vanity
feel itself entitled to expand. This was admiration, not for her accomplishments but for
herself, the triumph, not of a technical expert-
ness which any fat actress might win by hard
study at the age of forty and which her prudish dancing rival, Taglioni, had won in Paris
in spite of her long skirts and her skinny

calves. But here she conquered by her celebrity, her dash, and the charm of her sex upon a city of excitable, love-obsessed young men.

She basked in it, she expanded. The love notes, the tributes of platonic and political admiration rolled in with each morning's coffee in little baskets. The newspapers were declining Lola poetry in sheaves, because, as they tactfully explained, of the limited space allowance. But Lola knew she was furnishing her favorite weapon, a whip handle, to Pegasus, because she was getting sheaves of verse herself. And now and then the newspapers would print one of the better ones, such as *Fair Lola* in the *Herald* in mid-June

"I will not believe thee cold, heartless and vain,
   Man's victim thou ever hast been;
With thee rests the sorrow, on thee hangs the chain,
   Then on thee should the world cast the sin?
     No, Lola, no!"

Meanwhile, Patrick P. Hull, the brilliant young editor of the *San Francisco Whig*, who had come up with her on the ship from the Isthmus, was her shadow, and an extremely effective volunteer press agent besides. She was, with her real ability to cherish volcanic passions and publicity interests simultaneously, genuinely enamored of the huge, chivalrously pugnacious journalist of his era, with manners courtly enough for a Life Guard subaltern and a wit as keen as she had known in Paris. To make matters convenient, her bigamous marriage had been dissolved recently by the unfortunate Cornet Heald's drowning. The unregretted Captain James was at last dead of his Indian service maladies.

Free in the law and the sight of God, on July 2 she led the romantic Hull to the altar of the Mission Dolores and made him—was it, the wits asked, Count Landsfeldt? But the wits, as yet, counted only for advertising purposes. The governor was on hand with his suite for the ceremony and earned for himself more popularity by kissing the bride openly and appreciatively at the wedding breakfast than by many a well-planned political stroke.

But she had already touched new zeniths. With the stars of the San Francisco theatrical world, Caroline and William B. Chapman, Alexina Fisher Baker and Miska Hauser, a violinist of international repute, she had appeared in a benefit for the First Hebrew Benevolent Society on June 9, and carried away

the sensational honors from her longer established rivals.   On June 15, with the bill of
Yelva or the Orphan of Russia and *The Spider
Dance*, had come her benefit for the firemen's
fund.

Howard Engine Company No. 3 and Empire No. 1, in "full dress" uniform, escorted
her in a parade to the theater.   Thirty thousand dollars rolled into the firemen's treasury
from seats sold at fabulous prices.   When
word of this was passed around through the
audience, they rose to the royal mistress's acting with an uproar so continuous that in other
circumstances it would have been stopped by
the police.   *Yelva* passed with "continuous
outbursts of cheers" so violent that passers-by
hastened to the theater for fear of missing an
unscheduled political meeting.   But to the
pandemonium let loose when the *Spider Dance*
began, all this was only a discreet overture.

Down the stage rained the huge, bright-
colored helmets of the firemen, dozens of hats,
scores, hundreds.   In and out of the hail of
bushel-sized missiles, leaping around them and
over them as they fell in clusters and intricate
patterns of obstruction on the stage, stamping
spiders to death on their brims and in their

upturned crowns, the royal mistress wove her pageant of terror and furious gayety while the firemen in their gaudy uniforms stood up in the pit and yelled to high heaven.

The last spider died, the helmets were reclaimed and stuffed with flowers. Lola made her curtain call. San Francisco, she said, gathering helmets and bouquets gracefully to her bosom while attendants piled more in pyramids at her side, could only become the great or greatest city it was destined to be by having firemen to guard it. As for herself, she was happy to believe that she had the firemen's hearts as well as their hats.

For a thoughtful inspirer of revolutions the oratory may not have been original. But to a firemen's audience, proud of their record of facing an average of two holocausts a year and inflated with the sense of their city's metropolitan destiny, it was irresistible. The royal mistress kept the hats as well as the flowers. Also she remembered that, as the local representative of European aristocracy, it was her function to be exotic. Marie Gilbert of Limerick and Betty James of the Indian army spoke, according to the press, "with a slightly foreign accent."

The envious Chapman troupe retorted with a burlesque on *Lola Montez in Bavaria* and a "Spy-Dear" dance of engaging grotesqueries, but San Francisco stayed won. The press, still emotional, merely protested against making "a noble-hearted and generous woman the object of ridicule and scurrility."

The pet of a governor, married to a leader in the world of publicity and state politics, the idol of gallery gods, celebrity hunters and of the politically and socially powerful volunteer fire department, the royal mistress moved on the small towns and the mining camps in an effulgent sunburst of glory. In a lady born to extravagant vanities, no mood for such an approach could have been more unfortunate.

The first week in July Lola packed the devoted Hull among her baggage, enlisted the temperamental Miska Hauser for a side attraction and descended upon Sacramento. The state capital was already a considerable metropolis in itself,—just large enough to be violently jealous of San Francisco and the more violent because it was not quite able to have its rivalry taken seriously.

Consequently, reputations made in the port

were automatically suspect. In addition, the capital, while as frantically curious about royalty and European celebrities as any other station in the American hinterland, lacked the seaport's cosmopolitan tolerance for both foreign and temperamental mannerisms. It was prepared, no doubt, to relish an archduke or a royal mistress with abandoned ecstasies, but it demanded first that all foreign aristocratic distinctions be abandoned in deference to American democratic principles and that distinguished visitors submit pleasantly to the ordeal of being treated as "just folks." Sacramento must, in a word, be cajoled. And for Lola in her present mood of exaltation and triumph, cajolery was the most impossible of virtues.

On the contrary, when her first Sacramento audience showed signs of a critical coldness to the *Spider Dance*, she paused in the midst of it, and lectured them violently on their manners. Hostile observers even went so far as to charge that the lecture in its more emphatic stages became a torrent of abuse and profanity, but as they have left no direct quotations, they are doubtless open to the suspicion of prejudice.

In any case, the audience for several nights

dwindled away to a sulky handful, many of whom were said to have come provided with missiles and a bellicose desire to see the offense repeated. Meanwhile the proud firemen of the insulted city declined with dudgeon her offer of a benefit performance.

Lola retorted in her best brazen tradition by challenging the editor of the critical *Daily California* to a duel. She could right herself, her letter of challenge insisted, only by "inflicting summary justice upon all jack-a-napes. After such a gross insult (the *California* had objected to her manners and morals as well as her dancing) you must don petticoats. I have brought some with me which I can lend you for the occasion. I leave the choice of weapons with you, for I am very magnanimous. You may choose between my duelling pistols or take your choice of a pill out of a pill box. One shall be poison and the other not and the chances are even."

But in the nick of time the adroit Mr. Hull's diplomatic talents were brought into play. The countess withdrew her demand for the satisfactions of honor and the firemen reconsidered their decision. On July 11 the benefit took place, without showers of helmets but with all the other accessories of triumph. The countess took her curtain call with the handsome sentiment that "sunshine would always be in her breast when she thought of the noble city of Sacramento."

Afterward, to cement the peace more ostentatiously, three companies of charmingly uniformed volunteers marched in ranks to the Orleans Hotel. La Montez appeared on a balcony, seductively informal for a titled aristocrat, "without bonnet or shawl." There were more speeches and she tossed the firemen the flag which she had carried, she emotionally insisted, everywhere on her tour of the republic. Then, rendered extravagant by reconciliations, the helpful Hull proffered decisive civilities. He invited the three companies and their hangers-on to step into the bar and have a drink at his expense, "which," as the *San Francisco Herald* somewhat tautologically put it, "they did."

Nevertheless, harm had been done. Who was this countess, the suspicion clamored, who built her fame on the scandals of degenerate European court life and the cheers of the San Francisco hoodlums, and then used it to insult audiences of honest, democratic Americans?

Puritanism revived and suggestively inquired what was a royal mistress, anyway? Advanced Democratic partisanship took up the inferences and expressed its doubts of a foreign adventuress who had married a Whig editor and been kissed by a Whig governor.

Worst of all, Democracy's terrible humor had been aroused. If San Francisco had put the adventuress on a pedestal, the back country could certainly knock her off with a laugh. Indeed, the back country could laugh three times, which made it almost continuous. It could laugh in mockery of the airs she gave herself and thus shrivel her pretensions. It could laugh at the slapstick ferocity with which her vanity resented this preliminary ridicule. And if the tension of having a beautiful and scandalously famous woman among them had had anything to do with her elevation, they would strike her hardest by laughing at her allurement itself. The more she was desirable to their thronging, unsatisfied maleness, the more they would cure the ache of not being able to share her by loading her record as a charmer of men with burlesque and cynical ribaldry. They would make her undesirable, after the American fashion toward things of dangerous beauty, by making her a standing joke.

The process began at Sacramento where, in spite of the truce with the firemen, the ridicule grew. A new note began to creep into her press notices which undoubtedly reflected widespread opinion. She was no longer hailed as the noble-hearted revolutionary but suddenly she began to be exploited by humorous editorial paragraphers as another of those excitable foreigners. The glamor of her elusive royal connections and her fustian nobility passed overnight. After being greeted almost as a princess regnant, she suddenly saw her name given as Countess de Landsfeldt-Hull with a satirical emphasis and quotation marks around "countess." Her vogue as a serious liberal martyr evaporated in shouts of raillery, and on California dawned the shrewd and amusing certainty that the Bavarian intrigue was simply another exploit of an empty-headed adventuress.

Within a week, the state had taken her measure as accurately as Vandam and Paris, and with a far more malicious instinct to ridicule her and goad her into further absurdities, since it had to compensate itself for its sense of being buncoed. From a paragon of exotic charm and political virtues, she rapidly became an hilariously amusing combination of the comical stage foreigner and the crude social impostor, the natural butt of democratic and provincial jocosity.

Even fickle San Francisco turned from its devotions. Other favorites reigned already and the Chapman burlesque on her acting went on with gathering popularity. Editors pawed through the up-state exchanges for news which would delicately lampoon her. And it soon came.

As she went northward, audiences grew colder and her temper grew stormier. At Marysville late in July she turned on an assembly which had ventured to appreciate the talented Herr Hauser's playing more than her *Spider Dance* and abused it in a way which made her tirade at Sacramento seem like a gesture of friendliness. At the hotel the battle was renewed until the luckless violinist, scarified with words and threatened with the famous horse-whip, left the troupe. The inexperienced Hull, still flushed with the Sacramento victory, tried his stock of diplomatic oils on the disturbance and was taught the difference be-

tween easing a typhoon and feeding a confla-
gration. Ordered out of the "royal suite" for
all eternity, he went. The tour was over.

To Lola, however, the collapse of a theatrical triumph was simply another challenge.
As a retired dancer, she had upset a ministry
and provoked a revolution in Munich. Despite
gubernatorial kisses she could hardly upset the
good order of the state from Sacramento by
functioning as an official mistress. But she
could still astound and annoy and possibly ter-
rorize the Californians as a neighbor.

The last of the month the *Sacramento Union*
carried the significant personal item that "Lola
is going down to Grass Valley, Nevada City
and Downieville for mountain scenery, not
mammon." It was an interlude that was to
last three years.

Grass Valley was a thriving mining camp
nestling between pine-clad mountains and rapidly developing some of the pleasant essentials
of permanent village life. Here in the early
autumn Lola established herself in an attractive
cottage on Mill Street. The darling of romantic courts would prove her mettle to these

boorish Californians by leading the simple life.
There would be, and soon was, a garden, with
Lola working it in the most modish of Parisian
morning garments.

Only it must not be too simple. Lest an
international fame for wild audacities decline,
it must be a little savage, noticeably savage.
On fiery chargers and with a retinue of guides,
Lola hunted for days on end, with man-sized
weapons and some said in men's costume, the
big game of the mountains. The establishment
acquired an impressive assortment of terrifying
livestock: a fierce stallion, a biting and cursing
parrot, a ferocious mastiff and a pack of indifferent but horribly baying hounds, a bear
chained to the garden's entrance posts.

Tradition, indeed, even while she was still
in residence, made it two bears and then two
grizzlies, and added further that one of them
bit the calf from the leg of one of her temporary admirers, and that for yielding to natural irritation and shooting it, the victim was
banished on crutches at the end of the celebrated riding quirt. But it appears by more
reliable recollections to have been only one bear
and a mere brown one, tamed as a cub. Never-

theless, its mistress, enamored of savage appearances, pined for a pet puma which never came.

Too, the establishment of a woman of the world must have impressive touches. The royal mistress crowded the cottage with wagonloads of foreign, and therefore suspect, parlor ornaments. She loaded its cellars with strange wines and spirits. At first there seems to have been an air of condescending familiarity, almost of joviality, in her intercourse with the community. She laughed her best stage mirth when a miners' court solemnly tried the pet bear for hugging her and rendered a sympathetic verdict of acquittal. But this soon passed.

Grass Valley, already developing jealous notions of social precedence itself, was excluded from her doors, first by mere chilliness, gradually with virtual insults. Two nephews of Victor Hugo were unearthed somewhere in a prospecting camp and installed as house guests. Frederick Seward, son of the all-powerful senator from New York, was corralled on a grand tour of the west and subtly separated by Circe from the town's ambitious courtesies. Wandering political personages, traveling Europeans and strutting theatrical troupes all

LOLA MONTEZ
After Jules Laure

received this exclusive and flamboyant hospitality, but not the countess's fellow citizens.

So Grass Valley added to the general mood of ribald disillusionment a personal grouch of its own. It grumbled at her snobbishness and circulated scandal. Lola, with her usual cantankerous perversity, played up to it. The Methodist minister, catching the popular moral note after the manner of his kind, preached against her as a stage hussy and a scarlet woman of degenerate Yurupp. Attired in her ballet costume and followed by a train of jeering brawl-devotees, she stormed his door to prove to him that she was essentially modest. But Grass Valley was already so far gone in irritation and envy that it refused to see the humor of the performance. Not only the professed Christians, but the chronically unregenerate and even the bar-flies, backed up the minister to a man.

So the tension grew until the fall of 1854. Fourteen hundred young men milling about in a population of two hundred women began by hating a beautiful and unattached female for scorning them. They ended by hating her for being beautiful and unattached. Lola, as time went on, aggressively employed every chance to incense them further. What her giddy temperament quite evidently craved was to be recognized and adored as the capricious chatelaine of an American peasant village. Yet she was being railed at by non-conformist parsons, and met with black looks and guffaws like the village outcast. Could she drive her swaggering importance home to this canaille—she rolled her stock of French more and more resonantly as the town offended her with its grotesque Americanisms and even pretended at times on her shopping trips that she had forgotten her English—with a whip? At least if she tried she would probably enjoy it.

On November 21, the lady took her feudal pleasure. As has happened before and since with exclusive celebrities, there was one exception to the ban on visits from the neighborhood. This time it was Henry Shipley, editor of the *Grass Valley Telegraph.* If Shipley had not exactly the run of the house on Mill Street, he had at least the privileges of the front door. Some time earlier in the month he had been summoned there and instructed that his review of a coming ballet performance by a troupe of Lola's friends must be enthusiastic. The chatelaine gave him a drink and let him out with regal sensations of having secured a promise.

Consequently when Editor Shipley, as a conscientious journalist possibly perturbed about advertising receipts, gave the artists a satirical roasting, the "lioness" of San Francisco's greeting reacted in form. Either voluntarily or on a summons, Shipley went to the manor house to explain the misunderstanding and was ordered out, California rather than Paris fashion, at the point of a Colt. Next day, not unnaturally, the *Telegraph* edged into its enlightened foreign comment a reference to the "Lola Montez-like insolence and effrontery of the queen of Spain."

What happened next the *Telegraph* appropriately headlined: "Grass Valley Ring: First Fight of the Season." The "combatants," it described as "Marie, Countess de Landsfeldt, de Heald, de Hull, 'Lola Montez' and Henry Shipley, editor of the *Grass Valley Telegraph*. Time: 11 A.M. November 21; place, Golden Gate Saloon, Grass Valley; weapons: horsewhips, nails and tongue."

"First Round," the account continues: "Countess pitching in, strikes blow with whip. Shipley catches it—both close. Countess's second takes her off. Shipley falls back with whip in his possession.

"Second Round: Countess returns to attack —with her tongue. Shipley, provokingly cool, smokes his pipe and laughs at her.

"Third Round: Countess, urged to desperation, strikes at Shipley and spits in his face. Shipley magnanimously advises her not to go too far.

"Fourth Round: Countess tries on her old tactics—appeals to crowd as 'Miners, etc.' Crowd sensibly laughs at her.

"Fourth and a Half Round: A 'green' chap in crowd said something when countess informed him it was not his 'put in.'

"Fifth Round: Crowd greatly amused.

"Sixth Round: Cries of 'Speech from Shipley.' Shipley offers the stump to Lola. Countess informed Shipley that her name is 'Mad Lola.'

"Seventh Round: Countess reads extracts from *Grass Valley Telegraph*, counts number of words and informs Shipley that there are twenty words to be accounted for.

"Eighth Round: Shipley remarks that crowd has been sufficiently amused and concludes to retire in disgust.

"Ninth Round: Countess springs forward and demands the whip—'her father's whip.' Article in dispute placed in hands of disinterested party.

"Tenth Round: Countess asks all hands in to drink—crowd laughs and refuses."

But the honors of the combat were not to be exclusively appropriated by sports writers. That afternoon, before the tension had relaxed, the pen of the royal mistress undertook to finish what the riding crop had started. Readers of next day's *Nevada Journal* thus had, if not an unbiased account of the battle, at least an accurate photographic study of a noble heart in eruption.

Shipley, the countess fulminated, "a very commonplace being in intellect, of immense, overweening vanity," had broken his promise to say "nothing in praise or dispraise" of the visiting artists in order to glut his savage prejudices. Then, as if this breach of faith were not enough provocation, "a few hours after the door is burst open, my bedroom invaded with this Shipley's presence, he regardless of my sufferings, being in bed, a lady being present, threatens to cut my throat before he was done with me, using such language which I shall not disgrace my pen to repeat. I got up, took my pistol and told him to leave the house. He, still using to me the most offensive language, concluded to go. I told him that if he ever crossed the door of my dwelling, I should consider him in the light of a house-breaker and treat him accordingly. He left at last saying he would cut my throat. In my hurry to get him out of the house I helped him either with my hand or foot (in the hurry I forgot which). Mrs. M. says and declares it was my foot.

"I could not help laughing heartily at the exit of this hero of 1,000 battles which nobody ever saw or heard of but himself. The little nursery song of my childhood comes back to my mind of

> " 'He who fights and runs away
> May live to fight another day
> But he who is in battle slain
> Never lives to fight again.'

"This morning, November 21, the newspaper was handed to me as usual. I scanned it over with little interest, saw two abusive articles not mentioning my name, but as I afterwards was told, as having been prepared by the clever pen of this great statesman of the future and present able writer as a climax and extinguisher to all the past and future glories of Lola Montez. I wonder if he thought I should come down with a cool thousand or two to stock up his fortunes and cry 'Grace, grace'? This is the only attempt at blackmail I have been subjected to in California and I hope it will be the last.

"On I read the paper till I saw my name in good round English. The article will be in the minds of all the readers of this newspaper, of my barefaced hypocrisy and insolence. Europe, hear this; have you not found me too truthful, too bold, to say this? Has not the hypocrisy been on the other side? What were you thinking of, oh! Alexander Dumas, Beranger, Mery, and all my friends when you told me my fault lay in my too great frankness? Oh, friends, you knew not that Shipley lived and breathed—that his fiat had gone forth to the four parts of the world, and he had judged me at last to be a hypocrite.

"To avenge you all, I recollected the Woman's Rights Convention, took the benefit of Miss Lucy Stone's Principles, bonnet on head and whip in hand; that whip which never was used but on a horse was this time to be disgraced by falling on the back of an ASS.

"I went forth strong in the principles, as I have said, of Miss Lucy Stone and other strong-minded females, found this redoubtable man 'on the shoulder,' and, as quick as a flash of lightning, laid the said whip on his shoulder and head four times, on my word of honor, before my enemy could remember that he was sitting on a chair. The lady of the Golden Gate Saloon was sitting on one side, a gentleman on the other.

"After giving him four good whippings, he got up and squared himself on the most approved Yankee Sullivan principles, and was preparing to give me a stunner in the eye. The spirit of my Irish ancestors (I being a kind of 3/4 breed of Irish, Spanish and Scotch) took possession of my left hand, and on the most approved Tom Hyer principles, before he could attain my eye, I took his, on which—thanks to some rings I had on at the time—I made a cutting impression. As usual, this would-be-great shoulder-striker ended the combat with certain abuse, of which, to do him justice, he is perfect master of. Sic transit gloria Shipley. Alas Poor Yorick."

It was, in effect, her quietus. Grass Valley laughed, and as editorial shears sped the controversy from one newspaper to another, the whole state laughed. The unconscious humor of the countess's tantrums excited as viperish a mirth in the Californians as their descendants were to feel over the kidnapping of Mrs. Aimee MacPherson.

Yet with the courage of her self-satisfaction she stuck it out for six months. Mysterious letters were coming, ostensibly from Washington, about the plan of certain "southern gentlemen" to take California out of the union and make her its "empress." She doubtless believed them. It would never have occurred to her sublime assurance that the plot was preposterous, that the letters were probably sent by some California practical joker to tempt her into new absurdities, or that southern gentlemen on a still hunt for a sovereign would not recognize the difference between blood royal and a royal mistress. Quite probably she spent her last half year in Grass Valley in rapt expectation of a *coup d'état* that would give her as much celebrity with reactionaries as the Bavarian adventure had given her with liberals.

Besides, had not one of the letters mentioned
$50,000.00 for preliminary expenses?

But no revolution came, nor, probably, any
$50,000.00. So in June 1855 she sailed on the
bark *Fanny Major* for Australia, no longer a
chatelaine in a western pastoral nor a sex comet
from Europe, but a dancer with an income to
earn. A trifle ostentatious in her green parasol
and pink ribbons, she stood on the deck prepared for an ovation. But the crowd only
smirked curiously, and emitted a few wild
whoops, doubtless with pornographic undertones. California was not saying farewell to
the nobility but to a stock joke.

Nevertheless, the land with its crowding of
men must have drawn her, for she came back.
Once more in the summer of '56 she danced
her *Spider Dance* at the American Theater,
and played *Lola in Bavaria.* Once more she
saw them ridiculed and burlesqued, this time
with no defenders but herself. "If Lola
Montez as a politician can be relied on," said
the *Bulletin* wickedly, "the best form of government for Bavaria would be an old king with
a plebeian ministry and a foreign dancing girl
for counsellor of state"; and still more mali-
ciously found it impossible to criticise—"for

who could act like Lola Montez better than the
lady herself?"

At first she was icily scornful. She was ill,
she was grieving for the death of a manager
drowned in mid-Pacific. Emotionally, she was
inclined toward the tragic pose. But the tireless California jokesmiths refused to allow her
to hold it. An amateur humorist, signing himself "Country Joe" of the "cow counties"
dashed into the tragic atmosphere with a newspaper letter breathing righteous witticisms
against the *Spider Dance's* risqué eccentricities.
Lola, this stage purifier complained, "seemed
to get so excited like that she forgot there was
any men about there at all, and didn't see the
fiddlers right under her nose, once." A properly modest American rustic had to leave the
theater "afraid she'd take her dress right off."

The sensitive intimate of the Dumas circle
writhed with her usual furies and made her last
desperate effort to win a following. Of all of
her theatrical futilities, this is perhaps the most
amusing. The representative of the exotic
charms of the old world and the debased intrigues of European courts made her play for
the Native Americans. The Know-Nothing
party in 1856 was in full cry. It had a presi-

dential candidate in the field, a long list of
congressmen and senators sitting in Washington and was conducting an anti-Catholic agitation which makes the Ku Klux Klan's cru-
sade of the early 1920s seem like the uproar
of amateurs. Therefore, Country Joe must be
a Jesuit agent.

"It is beneath me altogether to reply to it,"
she wrote to the *Bulletin* next day in rhetoric
admirably adapted to Know-Nothing literary
modes, "yet when the viper does show its fangs
it is sometimes necessary to stoop and crush it.
Oh, Mr. Country Joe, you have shown yourself
the wolf in sheep's clothing, or in other words
the Jesuit likes not *Lola Montez in Bavaria.*
. . . Dear Mr. Jesuit, the *Spider Dance* is
merely an allegory. . . . The spider is the
Jesuit. The dancer is Lola the Jesuit-hater."

But the Native Americans were more inclined to look for wolves in foreign dancers'
petticoats than in newspaper contributors who
spoke their own rustic languages and prejudices. Nor did they care to see a sacred emotion
like Jesuit-hatred debased by being symbolized
in the revealing contortions of a foreign adventuress who had been a Catholic herself and
a Catholic sovereign's mistress. The Know-

Nothings, who had not seen many jokes since the inception of their movement, roared at this one a little louder and longer than their opponents.

Then quite suddenly she gave up the battle. In August she was willing to be the Joan of Arc of the Native Americans and no doubt still open to an engagement as a California empress. But in September she auctioned her jewels and announced her retreat into spiritualism. Did she fancy there might be a spiritualistic claque, or was her broken, humorless spirit simply seeking the release of a flight from reality? She left for the east in October without telling; and, by all her confused life's precedents, without knowing.

California heard of her once more, and ribaldry at her expense by now had hardened into a convention. She gave evidence in a debt suit in the east in 1858 on the character of a London solicitor,—and the evidence characteristically turned out to be chiefly autobiographical. She had spent, she quickly made it a point to inform the cross-examiner, two years at the court of Bavaria.

"Whom do you know there?" the examiner shot at her.

"Everybody but yourself," she answered with a flash of her old impudence.

"Were you the mistress of the king?" the exciting crucifixion continued.

"What!" said the countess, rising. "No, sir! You are a villain, sir! I take my oath on that book which I read every night, I had no intrigues with the old man. I knew the king, moulded the mind of the king to the love of freedom. I was engaged in political business. You might call me prime minister, if you please, or as the king said, I was the king. . . . I was on the stage, too, in Bavaria. It is easier to be a man's mistress than a dancer."

If she could only have been a jealous, prurient, sex-burlesquing male world's mistress all at once, she might have found such eminently plausible practical philosophy true even in California.

THE LAST LADY ROAD AGENT

ARIZONA by the year 1899 fancied it had made its world of sand, cactus and gila monsters reasonably safe for tenderfeet. This did not mean, of course, that the Arizonans were idealists in public service who surrounded each newcomer with armed body-guards or provided him with a license to get pugnaciously drunk without reaping the consequences. It merely meant that they had brought their civilization so far in line with the standardized pattern that the travelling stranger was practically as secure there in life, limb, peace of mind and physical comfort as he would be in Chicago or Kansas.

Between most of the important points in the territory he could travel on trains, and the trains were no more likely to be held up there than coming out of Omaha. If he settled in the towns, he found that the killers and the desperadoes, like Wyatt and Virgil Earp, early harriers of Tombstone, and Curly Bill of the New Mexico border, had either been politely extinguished by violence or driven more or less politely into exile. In either case they were remembered only by the oldest inhabitants, aged forty-five and upwards, and as remotely as Mexican war heroes.

Again if the stranger took to the ranch country he found that the fence wars were long over and that rustling was punished as vigorously and with about the same orderly legal processes as burglary in Phoenix. If he dashed to a new mining strike he usually found some large corporation there ahead of him patrolling the camp with its special deputies so that the fiercest of camp followers could hardly think of anything tougher to do than to annoy the company by serving as walking delegates to the miners' union.

Open gambling still existed but pot collection by the gun barrel was no more fashionable than in Buffalo. Moreover, the principal cities swayed ominously before rising moral agitations to have even this last vestige of western freedom removed. The saloon was still regarded as in nature but even there one was not scorned for preferring Manhattan cocktails and similar exotic mixtures to whiskey straight.

The territory, in short, was heading toward Rotary, golf and the sad conviction that school

board politics are as exciting as murder.   More,
it was proud of it.   But by all such tokens it
was due for an anachronism.   Pride in progress
is what stimulates the reactionaries.

This is a form of embarrassment from which
all communities suffer intermittently, as may
be indicated by the present archaic passion for
the bill of rights stirred up by the forward-
looking prohibition movement.   But the west
suffers from such outbreaks more often and
more violently than other regions for the west
not only breeds the normal proportion of reactionaries in the native population but it also
attracts and imports them in large numbers
from afar.   Even in the 1920s it is invaded
each year by thousands who honestly believe
that gun-toting, cowboy costume and dime
novel idiom should be its stock attributes and
who, so far as resoluteness in personal idiosyn-
crasy can accomplish anything, insist on reviving these hoary traditions, often with incredible flourishes.

Hence, it was quite in the pattern that the
reactionary who startled Arizona with a whiff
of gun-powder and a gust of old mannerisms in
1899 should have been barely ten years out of
a Canadian boarding school for young ladies.

It was not, apparently, a school of great exclusiveness nor, by British colonial standards in the Victorian era, of very adequate chaperonage. For slight, rather homely sixteen-year-old Pearl Taylor, who came up from her mother's home in Lindsay, Ontario, in the fall of 1888, was soon carrying on a feverishly clandestine affair with an attractive young rake about town named Hart. And since clandestine meetings were themselves incitements to recklessness, and marriage was only a name to her, she scandalized the school and left the principal to do some eloquent explaining by eloping with Hart in the spring of 1889.

For a time they floated about small Ontario towns where Mr. Hart derived a highly eccentric income as a racing tout and semi-professional gambler, varying this with occasional periods of steady work as a bartender and more frequent periods of drunken idleness. From time to time his wife grew annoyed at uncertain fare and Hart's hang-over tempers and retreated to her mother's at Lindsay. But on the whole Hart's charm held. When things went well with him he still had the glamor and the endearing mannerisms of the small town sport. In a sense, even the fluctuations of his fortune and disposition made life exciting,—which was an important point for a youngster who had just deliberately scandalized a boarding school. In 1893, when he went with several thousand other small town sports and touting experts to test the pastures of the World's Columbian Exposition, Mrs. Pearl Hart went along.

She suffered, of course, the now familiar disillusionment. Smarter bunco-steerers got the bulk of the rustic patronage and Hart was reduced to the ignoble employment of a barker at the lesser, and shadier, Midway establishments. Indeed, since this was obviously beneath him, he worked at it as little as possible and Pearl had to endure more starvation and abuse, more idleness and longer sprees than usual. As the fair closed, she decided to try another separation.

But Lindsay doubtless seemed a little dull after the ravishing sights of the Midway, and besides, Mrs. Hart had learned in Chicago of a new life. Half a dozen or more of the concessions on the exposition grounds had been setting forth for five months various exhilarating phases of the wild western atmosphere, and she had observed them all with growing infatuation. The land where men were men instead of small town tin-horns, where also they were obviously deferential, open-handed, expert in gunplay and personal heroism, and above all numerous, warmed such romantic fancies as the too sophisticating Mr. Hart had left intact. Also, she had come to know a considerable group of lariat experts, clay pigeon murderers and retired Indian fighters intimately,—some say compromisingly,—and had found them charming. So her ticket of release from Mr. Hart that year was bought to Trinidad, Colorado. Gossip hints, indeed, that an admiring show cowboy paid for it.

In any case, in Trinidad she found the west of the show representation considerably degenerated. It was still predominantly a man's world, to be sure, which meant that a young woman half-educated and untrained for business could find very little to do in it. But the coal miners, the ranch-hands and the two or three show cowboys of the neighborhood who made the town their winter vacation hang-out were certainly not interested in putting a footloose and rather unconventional young woman from the east on a pedestal. A few of them might have been willing to marry her if she had not had a husband already but as things were they were chiefly interested in conducting her by a series of rowdy convivialities into a life of dissipation. That, they argued, was what women who came out west without visible means of support or relatives to visit were for.

Pearl had not been noted for her social conservatism even as a boarding school pupil and her life on the fringe of the underworld with Hart had scarcely sharpened her sense of the proprieties. Now she was in a strange land, bitterly cynical about men and marriage, and rather anxious in the way of youth defiant to show the world how disillusioned she was. Besides, she needed money for bare necessities and the easiest way to get it was also the gesture by which she could most adequately express her contempt for an outrageous society. With a wry hilarity and a rather more hardboiled attitude than the average, Pearl plunged into the side of life which Trinidad's first families had learned not to consider respectable.

For two years more or less she drifted from one western town to another imbibing the secrets of a demi-monde that was rapidly becoming less pastoral and more sophisticated. She learned to drink with a stone head or not to drink at all when the situation demanded it. She cultivated the acquaintance of the few veteran killers and road agents who still remained unslaughtered or unjailed and learned from them a good deal about their trade operations. Then one day on the streets of Phoenix in 1895 she ran plump into Mr. Hart. He was the sort of gentleman, one fears, who, hearing that his wife was earning a little income informally, would show up to share it.

If so, he was in for a disappointment. Pearl was a little too intelligent to prefer dissipation as a permanent career and she was fed up with defying society. She insisted on settling down as Mr. Hart's good helpmeet. She got him jobs in various saloons and gambling houses, established a home and started raising babies. For a time the unstable husband seems to have enjoyed the novelty. But after the second baby arrived in two years he grew alarmed at the drain on his earnings and revived his old system of carousals varied with wife-beatings. Pearl stood it a few months and then gave Mr. Hart the relief he craved by packing the children off to her mother, now in Ohio, and going to work.

She did not, however, revert to her wilder phases but contented herself with the bonanza wages which a strong, capable young girl could make in the servantless western country as a cook in private homes and mining camps. Nevertheless, Hart followed her up, promised amendment as before for the sake of sponging off her, and again, with even more speed than usual, relapsed. She was wholly pleased when the Spanish War came along and this annoyingly plausible young man's patriotism carried him into it as a volunteer, so pleased, in fact, that she shocked the sentimentalities of otherwise sympathetic miner friends on several occasions by hoping the Spaniards would get him. When they failed, and he returned again as a deserving veteran, she wasted no time on the fancy that the war might have made a man of him but sent him packing out of her life for good.

She was in her middle twenties, she had seen enough of life to convince her that men and the social institutions were in a conspiracy to keep a girl who was doing her best to repair a romantic mistake of her adolescence, from

making headway.   She was in a mood to make
society pay for it and she had only her acquaintance with the lawless fringe of the declining wild western world to teach her now.

So it came about that as the stage from Benson to the new Globe mining camp was rum-
bling up-grade through Cane Springs Canyon
on the afternoon of May 30, 1899, the command suddenly came "Hands up!"   The passengers a moment before had noticed a man
and a boy trotting toward them around a curve
in the highway with the sleepy gait of summer
afternoon wayfarers, apparently with all the
leisure that comes of perfect innocence.   And
now the man and the boy had thrown down a
45 and a 38 on them and were obviously prac-
ticing the ancient and half-forgotten art of
road agentry.

But the passengers remembered the discipline expected of true westerners in such
emergencies and, at the man's orders, climbed
down for inspection along with their decidedly
non-resistant driver.   Meanwhile the boy got
off his horse and began going through their
pockets.

He was such a terribly little fellow to be

dragged into this criminal business, the travellers confided in relating their experiences at Globe that evening, that they almost wished there was some way of letting him off with a good spanking. His hard, sneering little eyes, his weatherbeaten round face and the tough way he drew his mouth down at the corners made them think he might be fifteen. But looking just at his size and his infantile plumpness, you would have said he was at least two years younger and maybe three. The impoverished victims carried away the definite impression that his grown-up sombrero, cheap trousers and suspenders did not become him and that he ought to have been at home somewhere in short pants studying his lessons. His father, or whoever the man was that was with him, certainly ought to get the rope or worse for leading a kid into a scrape like that.

But the "boy" was Pearl Hart. That spring she had been cooking at a mining camp called Mammoth and had struck up a more or less platonic friendship for a good-natured prospector named Joe Boot. Then Mammoth, in the nerve-racking manner of mining camps, was suddenly closed down and both she and Joe were out of jobs. Just at that moment fate had chosen that she should receive a letter saying that her mother, to whom she seems in her hard-boiled way to have been genuinely devoted, was critically ill in Toledo. If Pearl wanted to see her, she had better come at once.

Joe was taken into her confidence and together they tried to make some money by freighting other discharged miners' goods out of Mammoth. But the work was beyond her strength and collections were unsatisfactory. Next, they tried mining a prospect claim near the discontinued works but only discovered additional reasons why the Mammoth veins should have been abandoned. Then it suddenly dawned on them that Pearl must have her money at once if she was to use it at all and that the only way to get it was to help themselves to it.

Why not rob the Globe stage? Joe began urging this in their interminable conferences. After all, it was right in the neighborhood and was perhaps the only institution there that could be robbed without much elaborate organization to foil town authorities and certain identification. From his wealth of second-hand knowledge of the west of two decades

Road Agent

With Her Pet Wildcat

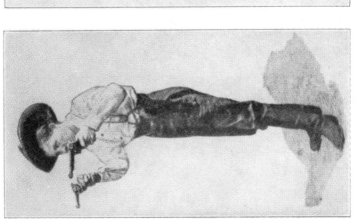

From "An Arizona Episode," Cosmopolitan Magazine.

Guarding Camp

PEARL HART

Obliges Her Public by Posing for Representatives of the Press in the Jail Yard

before, Joe argued that plenty of good men and true had robbed stages, gone undetected and made their stakes out of it, and in the end had been thought no less of by their neighbors because of it. It wasn't in the west's tradition to worry about the source of a man's money or a young woman's railroad fare if he, or she, was just careful enough not to get caught in the critical act. As for the fact that there weren't many stages left in Arizona and none of them had been robbed in a coon's age, that was all to their advantage. No one would be expecting road agents in May 1899.

So there they were at a conveniently forested turn in a mountain road robbing one, and it all seemed much simpler than even the hard-boiled Mrs. Hart had anticipated. The fat travelling salesman who trembled so that she could hardly get her hand in his pockets yielded up $380.00. A plaintive tenderfoot with his hair parted in the middle gave up $36.00; the driver produced a couple of ten spots and even a Chinaman assayed five. There was so much more than enough for a trip to Toledo that they actually gave their victims back a dollar apiece for bed and supper.

The whip cracked cheerfully enough and the stage drove off, leaving the last lady road agent and a too-protective prospector to face the problem of getting away. It was then, that in the inner consciousness they made a certain discovery which was to trouble them afterwards: the old wild west was dead except as a tradition of costume and mannerisms, and even in that tradition they were amateurs.

In a country twice as populous and therefore twice as hard to hide in as in the '70s, and much more likely to be shocked by a highway hold-up, they had robbed a stage without any arrangements for taking care of the proceeds and without any clear plan of what they would do next. The old-time road agents, with far better chances to escape pursuit and surrounding, would have had, like the Plummer outfit in Montana or Dunc Blackburn's gang on the Deadwood-Cheyenne line, a whole series of robbers' roosts to retire to and probably a pretty good fence and tip system besides. But Pearl and Joe had done their job with as much light-hearted swagger and carelessness as if they were performers in a wild west show. Surrounded by so much talk, dime novel literature and circus representations of "the good old days," they apparently had thought of their violent deed more as a smart bit of play-acting than as a serious crime.

So they trotted calmly up the main highway for several miles, not with any particular idea of putting on a bold front and appearing innocent, but simply debating where they should turn off. Finally, the bright conclusion was reached that instead of trying to put as much distance between them and their hold-up as possible during the first night,—which they could have done by heading northeast toward the New Mexico boundary and the Santa Fé railway lines,—they would try sticking around for a few days in the Cane Springs Canyon. It was a wooded, wildly mountainous district, they thought, with no inhabitants to speak of and plenty of places to hide out in the daytime. A posse would have a hard time following them into such jungles, and besides, they had heard that in a confused terrain pursuers could always be thrown off the scent by doubling back and forth on the trails.

So they took a right-hand by-path into this wilderness, which was even less known to them than to many of the public-spirited citizens of Globe to whom the robbery was just now being reported.　All the rest of the day they spent plunging across canyons at right angles and criss-crossing back again in ways which their amateur trail lore thought must be thoroughly baffling but which were hardly such expert maneuvers as honest riders or sophisticated road agents would have adopted. By night they had pretty well lost themselves and were rather horrified to come out suddenly on the Cane Springs road, not a great distance from the scene of the robbery.　Nevertheless, they followed it for six miles past the hamlet of Riverside and finally crossed the creek to make camp in a thicket near daybreak.　They hobbled their horses behind the bush clumps all day and slept.

Next night they pushed on, with characteristic amateur strategy, toward the railroad which, being the nearest line to the scene of their exploit, was being carefully watched for a man and a "boy" whom everybody in eastern Arizona now knew was Pearl Hart.　By good luck, they were scared out by some wagons on the road as they neared their own home camp of Mammoth and retired to the bushes for another day.　Joe even became so careless as to sneak into Mammoth that evening and got some tobacco from his cabin. But the best thing these resourceful desperadoes could think of doing next was to trot up to a sandstone hill back of the camp and hide for a day in a tiny sandstone cave. They had to kill a musk hog which was in prior occupation and, as the ventilation was poor, they choked all day from the powder-smoke.

They simply seemed incapable of getting a discreet distance from their well-known hangouts. And now the uncomfortable day in the cave had upset their sleeping schedule and their endurance was flagging. This fourth night they merely went as far as the school-house on the outskirts of Mammoth and after stealing a little hay for their horses and straw for their own bedding went to sleep in some bushes at the far end of a big field. Old-fashioned road agents often rode without rest for seventy-two hours on relays of horses, stolen or otherwise, to escape pursuers but this pair who were restoring the old western reck-lessness dropped from fatigue within a short walk of their own Main Street.

Refreshed, they went on for ten miles in the open daylight. They stumbled, not without horror, into an unknown Mexican settlement where Joe's spent horse fell into an irrigation ditch and was almost drowned. There was nothing to do after this but to rest their winded animals and they seem to have spent the afternoon cooking in a pouring rain in full sight of their Mexican neighbors. They were less than twenty miles from the hold-up and the whole country-side, full of spies and informers, to say nothing of the sheriff's posse, had had a chance to close in on them. When they rode all night over the muddy mountain trails their horses' feet made lasting imprints which were fatal. Just at dawn, they saw a mountain lion and, true to the western traditions which they honored with so much imperfect imitation, gave chase to it. Needless to say, in spite of much whooping and noisy shooting, the puma got away.

They went to sleep in a cactus clump in the foot-hills but, a little after the time for honest Arizonan breakfasts, were awakened by the yells of the successful posse to face the sheriff's Winchester. The little game of reviving road agentry was up. They had not had a chance to spend a cent of their hard-earned capital, and even the Chinaman got his five dollars back.

Yet Pearl Hart became a good deal of a celebrity over it. It was, from the standpoint of resourcefulness and organization, one of the worst stage robberies ever pulled, and the old-time road agents probably laughed over it secretly in their beards or in their penitentiaries. But stage robberies, good or bad, were getting so rare now as to be romantic. Furthermore, the old-time road agents, whatever had been their hardihood and efficiency, had never used women in their field operations. The public, especially the public east of the Pecos and the newly made Arizonans bursting with reverence for Stetsons and six-shooters, did not stop to reflect that this was because the old-timers had had too much sense.

So while Calamity Jane was drinking whiskey and passing into an ancient folk lore, and Cattle Kate and Belle Starr were dead and forgotten, Pearl was exalted into a sort of archetype of contemporary wild western womanhood. This was the land where men were men, every dime novel reader and cheap melodrama patron repeated to himself, and now it had suddenly transpired that women were likewise. If Mrs. Hart had not been shackled with various binding engagements with sundry Arizona jailers and penitentiary wardens, she might have made a modest 1899 fortune in vaudeville.

To do her justice, she played up to it more resourcefully than she had played up to her opportunity to get away with $450.00. She was jovial and masculinely free and easy with her captors. She wore her "boy's" costume of overalls and cowboy's shirt as long and as publicly as they would let her and looked very hard-boiled and carelessly defiant when the cow-towns turned out to see her at the railway stations. When eastern reporters began to call, as they did shortly, she had a pretty complete assortment of western dialect in the pre-Zane Grey manner which did not resemble at all her native Canadian inflections.

She was sportsmanlike, in the manner of the noble outlaws of old, with Joe Boot, insisting credibly that his troubles were all due to a charitable desire to relieve a young woman's distress. She was sentimental in the cow country's decently restrained manner about her mother's illness, although the edge was somewhat taken off this justification when that much tried parent got well. At length some admirer of her stoic virtues gave her a wild-cat

From "An Arizona Episode,"
Cosmopolitan Magazine.

Official portrait.

PEARL HART

A Real Lady

A Guest of the State of Arizona

kitten. To complete an effective allegory of the call of the wild as 1899 understood it, she made a cell pet of the creature and was completely acquiescent about being photographed with it. In fact, she was ready at any and all times to be photographed with rifles, sombreros, two guns drawn for either hip or shoulder offensive, or simply with the hard, steely-eyed look of the desert desperado of literature. Having been herself part of the gallery since the Chicago exposition, Mrs. Hart knew what the gallery liked.

In any case, to Arizona's delight, the prisoner required much moving around. The Benson residents enjoyed long discussions of the robbery with her, varied with expert testimony by local geographers as to where she must have gone in her flight. From Benson Pearl and Joe were taken to Florence, where the state penitentiary now is, by way of lengthy stops at Casa Grande and Tucson. Attention had given her the prima donna manner by now and she complained vigorously of the way the crowds stared. It made her wonder, she said, whether these same groups of steady gazers could have met her eye so courageously if she had dragged them out of a stage coach at the

point of a 38.   In fact, she was getting a bit
garrulous about the robbery and had, perhaps,
too much to say about how docile everyone
was to a little five-foot woman's bullying and
how amusing they were in their terror.

But neither boasting nor wild western atmosphere did her much good.   Late in June
she was separated from the faithful Joe and
transferred for trial to Tucson, where she
quite stepped out of her old-time hard character's rôle by trying to commit suicide.   But
since it was a very half-hearted effort and she
quickly recovered, one fears that too much
publicity had gone to her head and that she
felt this was merely an appropriate gesture,
on the melodrama heroine model, to compel
sympathy.   Instead, it seems to have affected
local sentiment disagreeably and in the fall she
got her sentence of ten years in the territorial
penitentiary at Yuma.

This put a good deal of a strain on the social
ingenuity of the institution since it had never
harbored a woman prisoner before.   But an
exclusive apartment was rigged up for her,
light work planned, and her stay proved more
agreeable than disturbing.   There were a few
difficulties at first because the guards lost in-

terest in watching the other prisoners and gravitated toward her cell and her working place with an hilarious enthusiasm that was hurtful to discipline. She seems to have had for men the charm of vivacious and comradely manners which homely but intelligent little women often learn to exert more effectively than their lovelier sisters because they must play up to masculine favor hard. But she kept her head and avoided scandal by quickly reducing the guards to the condition of harmless but emulously sympathetic boy friends. Barring the absence of the conventional social frivolities, she played in her little masculine world almost the part of a tactful college widow. It is even said that she advised her admirers wholesomely on their love affairs and domestic troubles, but she was wise enough not to use her power, as Belle Starr did, to seduce them into elopements and intrigues of escape. There was no Blue Duck gang for her to join if she should make her break and she knew the perils and discomforts of hiding out in the Arizona open country only too well.

With her fellow prisoners, on the other hand, her bearing was haughty and aloof. They were for the most part low-class Mexicans and town Indians, and could not have been especially congenial, while the prison discipline kept her rigidly segregated from the Nordic desperadoes as a delicate compliment to her sex attractions. But these regulations obviously pleased her or she would have found means to evade them. She was satisfied to maintain a sort of perpetual tea party for the guards and prison officials, while her shrewdness seized on the opportunity to represent herself as superior to the common felons in pathetic affliction. To strengthen this impression she became fervently, or at least ostentatiously, religious.

Such strategy paid. Before she had been a year and a half at the penitentiary chivalrous Arizonans were complaining that Yuma was a hell of a place to keep a woman for any crime, which, with its six months of infernal temperatures, it certainly was. There was a long procession of doleful rumors about her failing health, which were no less effective because of the fact that it seems to have remained miraculously good. Her conduct and technique were so edifying that she soon had most of the prison staff back of her application for clemency, and when she had served a little more than two years of a ten-year sentence, pathos won. She was released on parole and started at once, with a rather spectacular bit of moral heroics, for her mother's.

The west, however, had one more glimpse of her before obscure respectability reclaimed her. She was still a regional celebrity and when she stopped at a Texas city to change trains, she was annoyed, as before, at the slightly ribald curiosity of the multitude. An enterprising young man about town, anxious for an intrigue with what locally passed for eminence, professed sympathy and escorted her to the chaste seclusion of a saloon whose "family entrance" led to a maze of discreetly curtained booths.

I have the story from a waiter retired into capitalism in a near-by metropolis, whose gusto in the subsequent moral struggle has not flagged after twenty-five years.

"Jim flagged her," he said, "with all the food and drink in the house. She et like a starved wild-cat, showing, I guess, that they didn't feed 'em any too fancy over at Yuma. But all the likker she'd take was a coupla little glasses of sour wine.

"And every once in a while Jim'd try to get

real affectionate. An' then I'd hear her say, low and hissing-like but mighty fierce: 'Now you get over there on your own side of this here table an' stay there. I thought *you* was a gentleman.' An' Jim would git.

"Once I came in with some little order while this was goin' on and then I understood how Jim, who wasn't usually that way, was getting buffaloed. God, the look she gave him! It was hard as a killer's and mean as a plungin' bronk's. If a gal with those sort of lamping facilities couldn't make a success as a road agent, it was a pretty good sign the business had played out."

Eventually, it seems, Pearl came to a showdown. She switched suddenly from hardboiled to pathetic tactics, and told Jim that although she'd certainly not been good in her times, as everybody knew, she had sworn in her cell nightly by her crucifix that she would go straight as long as her mother lived. Jim melted in the approved manner of western roué sentiment and conducted himself for the rest of the banquet like an elder brother. Moreover, he saw her off to the train in the town's best hack and with the most chivalrously extravagant bouquet of lilies that had been procured up to that time out of season west of the Pecos.

Yet in retiring to the east and obscurity, Pearl Hart probably did the right thing for her fame as well as for her moral improvement. She was adaptable, no doubt, to the west's traditions of violence as few other women had been. But when that violence had become a tradition only, there was no fair chance for her to receive adequate training in its technique and her attempt to revive it as a reality was, even in 1899, a blundering anachronism.

New crimes were to come to the west with the motor and bootleg age, but they were, and are, the crimes of city underworlds rather than of open ranges. Their practitioners need little cow country sophistication but chiefly good constructive ideas of where to stow themselves at the cry, "Cheese it, the cops." Already in 1899, in spite of her youth, the last lady road agent was, to the passing frontier, a little quaint and old-fashioned. If she had tried it again, the glamorless west, fed up on dime novel heroines, would have taken her on as a stock joke. Having exterminated its male killers and bandits with civic satisfaction, it was in no mood to encourage desperate Dulcineas.

MADAME MOUSTACHE AND SOME GAMING LADIES

IT was light work, calling for deftness, intuition, tact and the more personal charm the better. It was performed in the west, under the bright lights and the most glamorous social atmosphere. Modish costumery was its chief convention. It was not dangerous except when one happened to be raided by an indoor bandit or to be caught in technical operations grossly inconsistent with personal honor. It made adventure possible to the sedentary and appealed to the love of excitement. It stirred the passions, but only those that were so sexless as to be virtually sex-protective.

Somewhat in this way I worked up to asking old Dan Spencer, ex-bartender of a score of cow metropolises and mining camps in Wyoming and Montana and philosophical authority on the last phases of the wild west in these regions, why there were so few women gamblers among the western adventuresses.

Dan was at first inclined to be conventional. Gambling was a "man's job," he said. That was all there was to it. Just like prize fighting or steer roping.

But it wasn't like these manly arts, I insisted. Dan had told me himself that plenty of ladies of ancient celebrity could manage a poker hand or deal faro and handle the dice and a keno outfit as well as a professional. They were certainly a lot safer than a man if they tried to crook anything. Then why, when they got tired of being mauled by men or wanted to make easy money and stay sober, didn't they go in for it?

Certainly the west's conventions would not have stopped them. Once a girl had kicked over the traces and showed she was not a tame house-cat, a school teacher or a bride from the east, any career open to her physical strength was also open to her talents.

"Well," said Dan, "I've figured it out this way. Most of the girls knocking around the towns in those days was too dumb to make professional gamblers and those that was smart enough would generally rather get the boys excited about *them* than about the cards."

I find this frontier Freudianism impressive. Most women of the adventuress class who came west on their own in the womanless era were drawn there originally by exceptional sex urges and vanities. Whether they were so drawn or not, they confronted on arrival mass attacks of male interest and admiration which left no room for other concerns. So, although promiscuity may have been a more casual and less profitable,—certainly for women a more dangerous,—way of earning a living than professional poker, it was emotionally more zestful and lots more fun. Why repel a potential admirer merely by proving that he could not fill an inside straight when it was possible to prove upon him with one's personal charms that gentlemen prefer blondes? Thus women gamblers remain rarer than feminine exotics of almost any other species.

Here and there one has added piquancy to some western community's traditions. But when you investigate you usually find that she played often and well but only for relaxation; or that she took a professional's place at Dempsey & Martin's one night in 1878 for a joke; or that she was a tin-horn's mistress for a period, possibly for a year-long cow town Odyssey, long enough to be remembered as hanging around his table and aiding him in his trickeries; or it turns out that she took up bucking the house rather hectically when she had grown old and her other resources for receiving pleasure were more or less moribund.

In spite of a somewhat shady class reputation there were male gamblers in the old west who lived by their technical skill and no other; who were, apart from their professional lives, neither liquor dispensers nor agents for other resorts, good husbands and fathers in some cases, and even church members. They were as wrapped up and specialized in their grooves as professors of the more abstruse sciences.

But the women invariably were adventuresses first and gamblers incidentally.

Still, some of them were the real thing,— when they worked at it.

The greatest and most famous of these stepped into celebrity from the northbound stage coach at Nevada City, California, one afternoon in 1854, stepped out of such complete obscurity that it was as though the vehicle itself had produced her parthenogenetically at the age of twenty-five.

She came from the south, so evidently at one time or another she must have made at least fleeting visits to Sacramento and San Francisco.

But whether she had been there for five years or a week, no man ever appears to have found out through any traces of a previous existence left by herself.

She declared herself French, and accent, mannerisms and fluent conversations in that tongue with mining camp sophisticates verified her. But neither she nor any other theorizer on her origins ever announced whether she was a native daughter of the west and some Canadian voyageur, some Louisiana Creole girl fled to escape a scandal, some belle of the New Orleans octoroon balls seeking to "pass" into white society in a new country, or a genuine adventuress off the Paris boulevards.

She announced herself as Madame Dumont. But no one ever learned who Monsieur Dumont was, or how or why he had been eliminated; whether, indeed, there had ever been a M. Dumont on the earth. It was simply that a young woman, charming and vivacious in the Latin manner and with a profoundly olive complexion, stepped from a stage and tacitly claimed protection of the California convention that one's past was nobody's business.

But the fact that she knew that convention thoroughly and how to take advantage of it and that she at once and completely adapted herself to all the other somewhat peculiar codes, customs and prejudices of a mining camp, proves something. Somewhere in obscurity she must have been on the ground studying her California for months, if not years.

San Francisco was, in fact, swarming with Frenchmen and more than one of the smaller centers had a Latin quarter of noticeable proportions. At the same time that the political commotions of 1848-52 were making voluntary exile attractive, the fabulous wealth and extravagances of California were holding out their lure to French cupidity. Frenchmen, and not infrequently French women, ran the more exotic restaurants and wine-shops, the exceptionally exclusive gambling houses, the more suave houses of prostitution. As wife or mistress, courtesan or overworked family daughter in some such establishment, Eleonore Dumont more than probably had served her time observing Yankee gullibilities, until her native shrewdness responded to the exhilarating unconventionalities of the local social atmosphere with the inspiration to go out and make a stake of her own. Whether she deserted husband, parents, paramour or patron in her plunge for freedom and fortune remains her own business after seventy-three years. But her more or less incognito flight to the northernmost camps of suitable size and prosperity at least intimates that her departure was not encouraged in the place she set out from.

Nevada City, however, where women were perhaps one to seven in the population in 1854 and where unattached, good-looking young ones hardly numbered one out of two hundred, received her with excited mystification. She was not affianced in advance to any of the miners, and she rejected all openings to become so within the first twenty-four hours. She avoided all irregular relationships, she did not go on the streets or into the town's flourishing vice district, and she certainly was neither a temperance worker nor a school teacher. She was gracious conversationally and made no snobbish demands for formal introductions before she would be friendly. But otherwise she stayed in her hotel, dressed in a slightly flamboyant manner as to jewels and décolleté, dining alone and locking her bedroom door each night like a lady.

Then in a week the mystery was solved. "The Madame," as the town was already call-

ing her in tribute to her slightly exotic flavor
and brisk little air of self-reliance, rented a
small store room on Broad Street and opened a
game of vingt-et-un.

The luckier and better staked miners made a
rush for her début, first getting out the stove-
pipe hats and dress clothes of solemn grandeur
that had done duty at southern plantation qua-
drilles and eastern college commencements.
The rank and file carefully refurbished working clothes, coon-skins and felt sombreros, and
edged in as shyly as a curious mob could.
Precedents were broken on the very first night
both in local attendance and more subtle matters.   For the first time in its somewhat event-
ful history Nevada City saw a game of chance
played by gentlemen with their hats off who
made no recourse to profanity even in exasperation.   Familiar topers were hesitant about
ordering the usual liquid refreshments and in-
veterate smokers about consoling themselves
with their customary tobacco habits.   The
Madame's place was not only orderly beyond
all local records—it trembled on the brink of
becoming ill at ease.

This catastrophe, however, the Madame
averted with magnificent tolerance.   "Zhee

bhoyss," she asserted with an enchanting cordiality, were all her "fr-r-r-renns." In her little house, therefore, they were to do as they liked, just as they did in the other gambling houses, or she would be *triste*, desolate, what you call broken at the heart. There must be no rough conduct, knife-fights, eye-gougings, gunplays, to be sure. But Madame did not need to ask this, since she realized that all her guests were there to respect her as a lady.

But just to show, for perhaps the first time in northern California history, that it was possible to be a perfect lady without being a Puritan, Madame herself sipped her portion of the opening night's champagne treats gaily and rolled herself cigarette after cigarette with the coquetry, but scarcely the inexpertness, of an ambitious ingénue. Between games the proprietress passed among her guests with a personal word of greeting for all, a bit of raillery here, a seductive pluck at the coat-sleeve there, a miracle of that astute general familiarity which women needing the patronage of large groups of men use at once to charm them and to keep them at their distance.

It was a technique in which a sophisticated Latin woman's gifts for innocently commercializing sex lure naturally shone at their best. Madame Dumont used it instantly and brilliantly to save the little game on Broad Street from becoming a public scandal on the one hand and from excess respectability on the other. Within a week, it was quite plain that the gallantly feminist little enterprise would not die when its novelty was exhausted.

Miners came to inspect the novelty, but stayed and came again because they had a better time at "the Madame's" than at the other gambling joints. The others might offer more varied amusements and, for the boisterously inclined, better prospects of thrills and physical outbursts. But the Madame playing her hands with the nonchalant sociability of a charming hostess, the Madame paying out her losings with droll little jests at her own inconsequential misfortunes and a certain tactful insinuation of delighting personally in the winner's triumph, the Madame raking in her winnings with grave courtesy yet with a sad wistful air of regretting that business had to be business,—the Madame was supplying emotional exhilarations which the surly efficiency and even the cultivated wit and good fellowship of the male professionals at Sam's or Jack's place lacked. Even when you threw in the prospects of debauchery, battle, murder and sudden death in which the more turbulent establishments specialized, the Madame's subtleties still had a definite edge. Seeing guns pulled and blood spilled over a card game was nothing unusual. But sharing a pretty young woman's naïve but sportsman-like emotional reactions to the conduct of Lady Luck certainly was.

Meanwhile because the Madame never slackened either in friendliness or discretion, and maintained her air of girlish exuberance as carefully as she did her skill at vingt-et-un, the charm of her place held and even grew. Miners began saying that they would rather lose to Madame Dumont than win from any male tin-horn in northern California. And they meant it. The near-by camps at Grass Valley, Dow-nieville and elsewhere sent delegations in droves to test out this unique delight of swell-ing the Madame's fortunes. Lonely prospec-tors, striking pay dirt off in the mountains a hundred miles away, rode in to provide her skill and independence with an encouragement that was both romantic and profitable. No game in northern California had such a con-stantly full attendance, such a long list of waiting applicants for seats, or such an impressed crowd of spectators as the Madame's vingt-et-un experiment. The fortunate young woman could have played twenty-four hours a day against emulous losers if nature would have sustained her.

French commercial talent naturally saw that a really tremendous opportunity was being but fractionally utilized. Alone, the Madame could only play vingt-et-un with the small group that could play vingt-et-un at a time. But all these waiters-in-line, all these curious, all these impassioned spectators would play something profitable to the house if only the Madame had the facilities. It was, of course, impossible to establish a house of women gamblers only. The Madame knew the social finesse required in that game and realized, as no doubt did the rest of Nevada City, that there was only one "Madame." Very well, she would remain the proprietress and the lode-stone of attraction while filling the rest of the house with professional males. Her beloved friends and so easily charmed guests could thus be losing to somebody while awaiting the ecstatic pleasure of losing to her.

Her choice for assistant receiver of the

patronage fell upon a young and charming but
thoroughly experienced gambler named David
Tobin. The youth was suave and presentable
and added strong masculine gifts of cajolery to
the Madame's feminine ones. He had, apparently, by recollections surviving down to a few
years ago, the combined manner of the ingra-
tiating salesman, the perfect sportsman and the
club entertainer. He took up his quarters in
the outer chambers of Madame's enlarged establishment, and there dispensed, with a growing corps of assistants, such amusements as faro,
keno and poker. The Madame's vingt-et-un
and chuck-a-luck operations further within
became a sanctuary for house favorites, the
larger spenders and for the fortunate few who
had braced the astute David's games to their
profit.

These happy conditions continued throughout 1855 until there occurred one of those
tragic separations which impress one with the
lack of business acumen among the intelli-
gentsia. Apparently love was not involved in
it, for both the Madame and Tobin were of the
cool-eyed, calculating type who kept their partnership on an even emotional keel. It could
hardly have been scandal since Tobin in amours

was a gravely discreet youth and the Madame was accentuating her virtue at this time almost to primness. Indeed, during her entire Nevada City phase she seems to have held her customers strictly to business by tactfully rejecting even the most respectfully amorous advances. When she left she was in a fair way to establish herself as a heroine of a miners' epic in the capacity of a sort of pucelle of the vingt-et-un table.

There was nothing to disagree about, in short, but the division of the spoils, and so Nevada City cherished for a great many years, without any evidence for it except the processes of elimination, the belief that this is what broke up the partnership. There was a slight falling off in the mining prosperity of the district toward the end of 1855 and possibly also in the population. Tobin, the legend claims, insisted on a higher pro-rata share of the proceeds which would have required the Madame to reduce hers and in effect accept a position as merely a kind of star employé in the establishment which she was famous for founding. Naturally, such arrangements were intolerable to Gallic commercialism and pride of enterprise and Mr. Tobin retired from the firm with a good deal of unpleasant French billingsgate sticking in his ears. Nevertheless his share of the profits constituted a stake large enough to take him back to New York and to establish a Tobin gambling house in that tolerant city, where, after operating on Civil War profiteers and successful politicians of the Fernando Wood and early Tweed rings, the canny David died in 1865 leaving an impressive fortune.

In the Madame, however, the change produced a new restlessness. By taking Nevada City at the full tide of its prosperity, she had made more money than the French girls who were wine room and restaurant helpers and courtesans back in San Francisco would make in twenty years. Nevada City seemed to be going into a decline but if she caught other camps on the rise and played them while the pay dirt was good, could she not double her money, triple it, multiply it even into one of the great California fortunes? So, early in 1856 the Madame set out on her travels. They were to last twenty-three years.

She tried the northern California camps first. But bucking the gold rush towns was different from settling in an established, con-

servative and, comparatively speaking, aristocratic little county seat like Nevada City. Men
gladly, almost sentimentally, accepted there
her pretensions to being a "good woman" even
though formal social recognition by wives had
to be withheld on the theory that a woman
gambler belonged necessarily to the underworld. But so long as she maintained her
poise, her standards were accepted and no questions asked. Drunkenness, any attempt at in-
decency or even incivility in the Madame's
place at Nevada City would have been repelled
by all her regular male patrons as quickly as it
would have been in their own parlors.

But in the rush camps more often than not
the spirit of "what the hell is she here for?"
prevailed. Many of them were controlled by
the roughs from the first, which meant no
effective policing and that no woman's reputation or even her physical security would be protected if her occupation connected her at all
with the camp's communal gayeties. The
tougher element among the gamblers, jealous
of the Madame's success and peculiar emotional attractions, were increasingly anxious to
drag her down from her pedestal by involving
her in the life and customary scandals of an

underworld, which served too much as a foil
to her exotic and sedulously exploited chastity.
However much Madame Dumont tried, or did
not try, to maintain her Nevada City discre-
tions, she was forced to make her way against
a gathering storm of obstacles and temptations.

Once we catch a glimpse of her flashing out
against it all at Pioche in the late '50s.   All
the roughs in camp one night invaded her
rooms, drunk, quarrelsome, flourishing re-
volvers.   They intended no harm to the
Madame personally, no doubt, but evidently
they were quite willing by their conduct, which
was as obscene as it was boisterous, to give her
house the reputation of the most disorderly
gambling hall in camp.   In Nevada City the
first drunken disturber would have been thrown
out by mass action even before it had broken up
the sacrosanct twenty-one game.   But here her
lone bartender was helpless.   The Madame,
however, rushed out and scolded them humorously for acting like bad boys out on some Hal-
lowe'en expedition to scare helpless old women.
Did they think she was the kind of an old
woman to be scared by their frowning false
faces and their loud alcoholic noises?   If they
did, they didn't know their Eleonore Dumont,
—she who understood that bad boys would be

bad boys until they chose to grow up and pretend that they were gentlemen and her friends again.

This Gallic ridicule addressed with appealing sleeve-pluckings to the ringleader sobered and disarmed them and they departed after an orderly exchange of drink courtesies. But hardly always could tact have been so successful. In other and possibly more rowdy camps there were disturbances in Madame's place which could not be quelled. There were indignities. Hardly a censorious soul to begin with, loving crowds of men and their antics, the Madame was not always on her guard. She had, for instance, in Nevada City stuck to her temperate wine drinking. But the crowds of men went in for the neat consumption of whiskey and brandies almost as a ritual of their vitality and maleness. The Madame, to show that she was a sport, would go with them.

More than once the Madame was a little dull in her play, a little boisterous, a little careless in her once immaculately edifying repartee. There may at times have been knock-out drops, for the rival gamblers in the worst camps were capable of it. At any rate the life was, while free and in a sense a little heroic, coarsening and degrading in most of its constant associa-

tions. And it is possible, too, that the earlier
attitude of extreme propriety was a pose only,
adopted by the Madame after years of sophistication in the San Francisco tenderloin had
suggested to her shrewdness that it might have
commercial value. At any rate, it was common
knowledge in the northern California camps
before 1860 that the Madame no longer invariably disdained to make money otherwise
than at the vingt-et-un table. Moreover, as
time went on there were particulars and an increasingly open profligacy.

There were hardships, too, which were not
favorable either to charm or to morals. Rush
camps were invaded which offered nothing to
rush for, and the Madame would be out the
expenses of her lavish traveling comforts and
of installing the luxurious gambling equipment
of the times all for nothing. There were times
when she sought to recoup these losses by bucking the games of other professionals with her
shrinking capital and the rivals were not, as a
rule, inclined to be generous. Time and again
the Madame made and lost fortunes no doubt
as bounteous as the comfortable one amassed at
Nevada City. But she also knew privation.
She knew exposure to the mountain weathers,

the primitive conditions of trail and camp life
and to more and harsher liquors.

It was not good for the swarthy Latin type
of beauty which ages and wrinkles early even
in shelter and luxury. The Madame was
hardly thirty in 1860. Yet her trim little
figure of Nevada City days was already fatten-
ing to grossness. Her complexion was rough-
ening and seaming a little with dissipation, her
eyes were losing their dark, girlish coquetries
and acquiring the beady heartlessness of middle-aged French women of the mercenary
classes.

Worst of all, the thin little line of down
which had been noticeable on her lip in girl-
hood almost as an exotic adornment, was now
growing with a typically Mediterranean luxu-
riousness. "Madame Moustache" men began
to call her with their terrible western gifts for
mordant nick-names. Though none dared call
her so to her face it was the sign of her arrival
at the estate of a regional notoriety. But a
little while ago she had been a delicately cherished celebrity without being notorious at all.

The gold rushes led into wilder and wilder
regions and Madame Moustache followed

them.   She was an early arrival in the camps
on the Nevada desert and shared in the revels,
and profits, which accompanied the opening
of the Comstock lode.   She trudged north
through the roaring and villainous ghost towns
of Idaho, where characters who had learned the
last refinements of thuggery in California came
to escape California's increasing restraints.

Always she held her own in these strenuous
environments; she asked no quarter for sex or
for novelty.   Now and then she astonished even
the blasé western underworld with her feats
of commercial astuteness.   Once in the raw
camp which has become Boise City, when the
miners were strapped after their first pickings
of surface ores and all the gamblers, including
herself, had been ruined by bucking the games
of some slick, fly-by-night strangers, she performed the incredible legerdemain of raising
$1,000.00 within twenty-four hours and start-
ing her establishment just as the town got its
second wind.

In a more remote Idaho camp, near the present Blackfoot, she is said to have uncovered
the schemes of another group of professional
fleecers and, by the sheer bluff of her hardness
and one of her rare Latin rages, to have com-

pelled them to decamp and give up their ill-
gotten profits. Many a rough, ready for disturbance, hold-ups or worse wilted at the touch
of her professionally appealing hand on his
sleeve, and her command of suspicious geni-
ality: "Sit down and behave yourself, my
friend, or out you go." Legend has it that she
thus subdued even the ferocious and half-mad
Boone Helm of the Plummer gang on one of
his rampages and yet retained his friendship
and his patronage. Apparently, however, her
contact with the Plummer outfit occurred during their approach to Montana through the
Idaho and eastern Oregon camps for there is
no record of her being in Alder Gulch during
the period of their outrages. But by 1864 she
was in Bannock, where her place is still remembered as a long, log house with four rooms
downstairs and second story apartments.
There was her little bar, her dance hall, still
her own private chamber for the beloved
twenty-one game and a larger apartment for
keno, poker and faro players. But though
gambling was still her first love and her main
interest, Madame Moustache had descended to
much that Madame Dumont of Nevada City
days would have scorned with dignified blushes.

Three camp grisettes were installed in the dance hall and the second story as insurance that lucky miners would not spend their earnings elsewhere. A little later she had the strapping, fifteen-year-old Calamity Jane in tutelage.

Four farm boys travelling up from Utah to sell eggs to the poultryless Montanans kept, nevertheless, rather pleasant memories of her all their lives. The miners invariably romanticized her, they discovered, because, once she had won their money, they could eat and drink at her expense indefinitely or count on her for stakes on the wildest prospecting ventures. The boys themselves sold their eggs to her at the profiteer's price of $1.50 a dozen without arousing a single Gallic protest. In her way, too, she mothered them. The more advanced whiskey-drinkers of the group were encouraged to take cigars at the bar as soon as their slight alcoholic tolerance manifested itself. One youngster in particular who drank cider she honored by sticking to that tender beverage herself through all the rounds of a somewhat ambitious wassail. When the wiles of the girls in the establishment stirred the young visitors to bashfulness rather than the expected reactions, she called the hussies off and gave them a guitar-playing and jig-dancing party as innocuous as a church sociable among their neighbor Mormons.

Even so, before they left they saw her harder side. A Scotchman named MacFarlane coveted the place and the command of her still buxom charms which had been enjoyed for several months past by her male agent and factotem, one McHarney. Carefully filling himself up on the Madame's whiskey one night, MacFarlane ended the rivalry with an accurately placed revolver shot.

The dead man had been a faithful worker and, as such relationships went in the underworld, a genuinely devoted lover. Yet the Madame merely had his body removed to a small alcove, called the coroner, bailed out MacFarlane for a thousand dollars, while the games and the dancing went on. Less than an hour later, MacFarlane finished his formal interview with the police authorities and inherited the job. He wanted it, knew the run of the house. This was the Madame's viewpoint; therefore he ought to have it. Twelve years later she was still able to laugh at the remembrance with Gascon cynicism. It cost her a hundred dollars to get MacFarlane out of his difficulties, she admitted, and this was very triste, because "Meestaire MacFarlane" proved not to be worth it.

Nevada claimed her again for a hectic summer, and some time in the late '60s she seems to have followed the construction camps of the Union Pacific through Wyoming. Somewhere in this period her northern California admirers heard, and apparently believed, the report that she had amassed a fortune, bought a farm, settled it upon a scamp of a husband who promptly sold the real estate while absconding with the cash. Her generous side might have been capable of it, but place names and documentary proofs are lacking and her French commercial guile is certainly against it. Quite possibly it was her favorite explanation for the brief period when she attempted to queen it in the San Francisco demi-monde as proprietress of an establishment for French women only where gambling was distinctly not one of the amusements. A lady ostensibly devoting her career to the moral science of vingt-et-un naturally would have had an impressive alibi for a lapse which evidently ended, besides, in commercial disaster.

In any case, she was in Cheyenne in its great days, in the middle '70s when Wild Bill stalked the streets, the bride-groom of Madame Lake-Hickock of the circus, and when the clans gathered for the Black Hills rush.   She was in Deadwood herself with the "seventy-sixers" and back again for a brief and apparently unprofitable stay with her paraphernalia in 1878. Meanwhile, in '77, Eureka, Nevada, was cheered with her presence, where in a two-story edifice of some magnificence she received guests, jewelry and a huge gold brooch blazing over her black silk evening gown and the moustache looming over all more savagely than ever.

Fittingly, too, Bodie called her at the last,— Bodie, standing to-day above Lake Tahoe uninhabited but the most immaculate and complete of ghost towns, kept like a public monument. But in 1879 Bodie saw the last reunion of the forty-niners still strong enough in muscle, wits and drinking capacity to raise hell.   They raised it with the fervor of old graduates, with the snorting pride of finished competence, the self-conscious determination to make the most of a last licensed indulgence until the announcement "I'm the bad man from Bodie" became the stock witticism of Main Street rakes and professional parlor cut-ups in Bangor and Savannah.

But the pace was too fast for the Madame. One morning early in September they found her body by the road two miles from town, and a bottle of poison lay beside it. There were no notes, no explanations, no pleas for sympathy. Whatever her less savory enterprises may have been, the old gambler died true to the etiquette of the profession.

They had broken her bank, but this could hardly have prompted her. It had happened too many times before and the genius which had raised a thousand dollars in a night at Boise was by no means fled. It could hardly have been love, for the Madame was immunized to its more disturbing temptations and disappointments by habit of mind and long experience. It could hardly have been liquor, though the Bodie brews were vicious and plentiful above average. The Madame knew these toxins too well to be bowled over by the emotional depression of a chance hang-over.

But the Madame retained one of the self-destroying vices. Unlike Calamity Jane, who grew old with a boisterous acceptance of the humors of decrepitude, or Belle Starr who grew dowdy in half-savage contentment, the Madame was vain. To the last she conducted herself as though the charm and beauty of her Nevada City days were still potent.

Perhaps one of the impish old rounders at Bodie had called her "Madame Moustache" to her face.

AND OTHER WILDCATS

DID the Madame have competitors? Unquestionably, but not serious ones.

Apparently she never came to the southwest, but in the early days of American penetration there Mexican women who were monte sharps were so common that they acquired no individual celebrity. In Mexican society, however, the line was thinly drawn between patrons and professionals, or rather almost everyone played as a professional after work, when out of employment, on fiesta days or when it rained. Girls in the border pleasure resorts often ran games in the early evenings to add to the house's popularity and their own earnings. On the other hand, women of good repute often on community social occasions and sometimes as a permanent enterprise ran small monte establishments as a means of supporting excessively large families including, as a rule, ornamental but expensive husbands. Now and then some old crone who kept her wits about her found it more profitable than chile-raising or tamale-vending in the plaza market. According to Col. Charles D. Poston, American bachelors in the settlement of Tubac, Arizona, in the '50s and '60s lost regularly a sizeable proportion of their incomes to their Mexican washerwomen, who, inspired no doubt by the Yankee vernacular of misfortune, nicknamed their Nordic patrons, "los God dammes."

El Paso, too, in the last turbulent twilight of open gambling had a sportswoman of unforgettable piquancy though hardly of the Madame's epic performances. She was Minnie, the companion of no less a person than Colorado Charlie Utter, impresario of Wild Bill's and Calamity Jane's descent upon Deadwood. Charlie was well up in his fifties when the 20th century opened, but his blonde ringlets and his statuesque "old partner" poses were as impressive as ever. Also, apparently, his taste for individuality in feminine flamboyance was unshaken. For Minnie by voluminous local testimony was barely four feet tall and dressed always in the height of Parisian fashion.

She was an expert poker dealer, by all accounts, and served honorably and efficiently in a number of El Paso's chance palaces at regu-

lar men's wages. However, she did not, like
Madame Moustache, aspire to personal pro-
prietorship of an establishment and merely
worked in order to help Charlie, whose delight
in leisure was increasing with age, maintain
his natural state of splendor. When the El
Paso Armageddon was finally won by the
anti-gambling reformers in 1904, Minnie and
Charlie quite sensibly decided to abandon a
republic which no longer appreciated their
talents and to pool these in a medicine show
for the benefit of the ailing Mexicans. For
years they travelled profitably through General
Diaz's land of moral freedom, dispensing
health and card tricks until at last they penetrated Central America. There Charlie died
of a fever. Minnie, however, survived many
years in Los Angeles with a sufficient fortune
to maintain her distinctions of toilette to the
last.

Elsewhere, too, such purely local celebrities
seem to have flourished and on the outskirts of
Deadwood Poker Alice still lives. But in spite
of her many merits Poker Alice appears to belong to the type on which spurious legends of
gambling Amazons are founded. Often in
the bold, wide open days, she strolled into some

gaudy sportsman's paradise and broke the bank in sheer delight of pasteboard battle. Often in her own houses of entertainment after the serious pleasure of the evening was over she has refreshed favored friends with games which have put a considerable strain on their credit if not on the friendship. But although her zest, skill and fortunes are properly famous, Poker Alice has functioned only as a patron of professionals and,—a tactful hostess.

Only once by even so much as a tradition did Madame Moustache encounter a formidable rival in the flesh. In Deadwood, local legend tells, she greeted Kitty the Schemer with the hauteur of a Daughter of the Confederacy regent acknowledging an introduction to a mere member of the Ladies Auxiliary of the G.A.R.

Kitty had advanced upon Deadwood in 1876 with the information, startling to tenderfeet, that she was queen of the gamblers of the San Francisco Barbary coast; that when business slumped in that triumphant seaport it was her practice to sail for Hong Kong or Yokohama and open a gambling hall that was famous throughout the cosmopolitan orient; that just now she was running her small poker and chuck-a-luck game in this lowly Black Hills village merely to break her journey to the diamond fields of South Africa.

The Madame merely shrugged her shoulder, pouted the moustache and announced: "I have never had the honor to hear of Kitty the Schemer in California." The blow was a severe one to Deadwood pride. But the Madame in her less lady-like but more confidential moods went further and proclaimed that Kitty was a plain liar.

Since San Francisco apparently had not heard of Kitty the Schemer by the summer of 1927, I am inclined to believe that the Madame was right.

THE CLAWS OF RESPECTABILITY

BUT respectability, too, ran a little wild.

The same atmosphere and freedom of the west which stimulated feminine folly and feminine malevolence to almost virile forms of expression also released the economically predacious and the reforming passions of women for much explosive flamboyance. "Ladies" were rare west of the Pecos, even if, as the west did, we accept the word in its biological rather than its social implications. A "lady," therefore, was stared at, admired, deferred to, and when in the slightest degree physically appealing, was mooned after as scarcely had happened since a certain famine in erotic facilities brought on the rape of the Sabines. From 1849 until the first decade of the 20th century much of the west lived in a state of potential polyandry which kept feminine vanity and self-consciousness, the womanly instincts of dominance and lawlessness constantly near the point of outburst.

Temperamental excesses were encouraged meanwhile by a society which was extraordinarily tolerant of conduct and personal idiosyncrasies even in respect to its males. Indeed, it is possible that the range and mining states were kept from relapsing into matriarchates not so much by constitutional guarantees of a republican form of government as by the fortunate circumstance that most of the western Circes were too isolated from each other and too occupied with cooking for ranch hands to bother with politics.

As it was, nevertheless, the woman who failed to be courted and indulged in the west usually was fit, as a specimen of pulchritude, only for museum exposure. Passable women who had the leisure and the receptive qualities to grasp the import of their charm and to sense their exaggerated social prerogatives usually determined quite accurately that whether for crime or for virtue, for pleasure or profit, a "lady" could get away with murder. The west's somewhat garish record of slaughtered erring husbands and of red light district killings unaccompanied with convictions or even prosecutions shows that hundreds literally did.

Naturally on women of quick intuitions surmises of the new state of privilege dawned by more or less occult processes the instant the lands of congested virility hove into sight. One Albert D. Richardson who wrote an entertaining work for our grandfathers, *Beyond the Mississippi, 1857-67*, cites the possibly apocryphal but highly symbolic case of a certain Mrs. William Arthur as far back as 1842. Missouri was the "man's country" then, and immediately on crossing the Mississippi, Mrs. Arthur redoubled the censorious zeal for her husband's moral improvement for which she had already been famous in Indiana.

Arthur bore it for a day or two with becoming patience. But he found that he received far less sympathy from his new male associates than he was accustomed to finding among the relatively civilized Hoosiers who valued women with some sense of proportion. Then, when patience availed him nothing Arthur with every appearance of despondency went swimming in the river. He dove from a tree bough with his usual flawless facility and swam toward deep water. Then much to the annoyance of a mate who was just beginning to learn what a victim was good for, he sank, and ostensibly failed to come up again.

Mrs. Arthur wrung her hands and ardent males consoled her by diving for the body. But meanwhile the crafty fugitive had swum under water, come up behind a log and made his way to the Illinois shore and the emotional safety of a fairly even sex ratio. Eventually, with the help of a "confidential friend," he made his way back to Indiana and remarried. Mrs. Arthur, it is to be presumed, stayed on the frontier where men might be men, but women were ipso facto goddesses.

The feminine lust for power did not, however, confine itself to male victims. In Custer in the Black Hills in 1877 a woman of the town's conventional strata had one of the frailer sisterhood up in court for bathing in the creek within fifty yards of her house. This was considered unnecessary exposure in the judicial sense and the culprit was fined fifty dollars. But within a few days the same defendant was brought up by the same plaintiff for performing her general ablutions at a distance of two miles. That seemed a reasonable distance to preserve mutual privacy, the court objected. But the reformeress insisted that civic propriety had been outraged because she had been able to see the offender with opera glasses.

Not all the reforming ladies, to be sure, conducted themselves with this splendid violence. Woman suffrage was put over in Wyoming in 1869, not by extravagant oratorical orgies, jail-courting pickets, front page publicity stunts and the hectoring of territorial governors. A small group of plausible but home-keeping gentlewomen merely made it a point to convince an influential member of the territorial legislature over the tea-cups that their voting privileges were worth fighting for. He received the inspiration essentially in good faith, though also apparently, as a recently reconstructed southerner, with the pleasant thought that giving women the ballot would be a mildly humorous way of paying back the Yankees for having given it to the negroes.

True, too, the backwash of the temperance agitation of the '50s reached California without prompting any memorable feminine ferocities. A certain Miss Pellett traveled the state intensively in 1853 and 1854, lecturing profitably on the joys of abstinence and the kindred therapeutic science of hydropathy. But although the newspapers made much of her "strong-mindedness," they also often found occasion to commend her for being young and comely. In fact, so little of the virago was in her that when the question of her free speech prerogatives was raised at a public gathering in Downieville, she stood modestly aside like any other well-bred Victorian débutante and let two young men of the town fight a duel about it. And when a waggish stage driver deposited her and a young male champion of hydropathy at a notorious Spanish dance house instead of at the hotel in one of the less refined mining camps, she won the good opinion of a hostile audience by telling it as a good joke on herself. Naturally there were ladies of equally evangelical piety in California who insisted that Miss Pellett had been lured west not so much by her zeal to charm men to temperance as by the hope of charming them to herself.

Nevertheless, in the long run the atmosphere of adulation and constant curiosity in which women lived in the west as a sex made it almost as difficult for a good woman to restrain her goodness as for a Calamity Jane to

content herself with being innocently hoydenish. Although the old west had largely passed
before militant female virtue amazed the
world with its most spectacular explosion, the
fuse was laid and ignited in a time and a social
situation in which violence was peculiarly a
"lady's" privilege.

A NOTE ON CARRIE NATION

PERHAPS the greatest sociological error yet made in respect to the outstanding Joan of Arc of the prohibition movement has been the effort to appraise her as a phenomenon of mid-western righteousness; as the logical, albeit somewhat florid, product of the Kansas of orderly pietism, established Puritanism and habitual village intolerances. Actually, Carrie was frontier,—frontier in environment, frontier in sophistication and above all frontier in technique.

As evidence to the point I submit that both before and after Carrie smashed the glass heard round the world, the middle western villages, the eastern urban centers and all other regions of the republic where the social conditions of the "wild west" had never penetrated, swarmed with prohibition enthusiasts quite as fanatical or quite as mad as she was. But did any of these daring apostles of uplift ever devise campaign tactics more unconventional than sighs, prayers, scandal-mongering, oratory, statistical extravaganzas and political lobbying?

On the contrary violence and typically feminine lawlessness were first brought into play as
weapons of war and publicity precisely in the
region where as late as the previous decade
women had been practically above the law because of their scarcity and where the frequent
shooting up of saloons by customers and the
personal enemies of the bartender had been
regarded as a mere manly peccadillo. Moreover the woman who achieved the gaudy in-
novation of brickbats and hatchets in holy
warfare had been herself in contact with such
an environment for the greater part of her
mature life.

Carrie, to be sure, had been born in Kentucky in 1846. But just before the Civil War,
in her most impressionable years, her parents
had taken her for several years to Missouri.
There in the late '50s social conditions in the
hamlets and backwoods districts already ap-
proximated those of the range and mining
camp country in many respects and there a
larger crop of future desperadoes, good and
bad, male and female, was being raised to the
acre than in any other section of the republic.
Toward the close of the war or immediately
afterward the family spent some time in Texas.

Here, again, the disproportion of women in the population, the lawlessness of a new country and the disorders of reconstruction were as favorable to feminine emotional instability as were similar elements in Alder Gulch, Montana, or in the Wyoming army posts.

Carrie seems to have been a comparatively finished product of her environment when the family made a brief return to Kentucky, probably in 1866. With an exaggerated sense of her sexual importance she forced what was morally a shotgun marriage upon a young physician in the household who had committed the heinous crime of kissing her in a dark hallway. Once in possession of the victim, she promptly and intensively proceeded to nag him into acute alcoholism and to gloat over his early death from this cause as the fruit of his wanton disobedience to her proper authority and a sort of left-handed compliment to her superior righteousness.

This tragedy disposed of, she quickly appropriated another bridegroom, one David Nation, an itinerant lay preacher. In the late '70s, again by way of Missouri and the now wildly western southern Kansas, she was back in Texas. She spent ten years or more there, enjoying the privileges, of a religious eccentric with much the same defiant flamboyance which Calamity Jane displayed in cultivating the eccentricities of bawdiness. Dismissed from the Methodist and Episcopal Sunday schools of Richmond for certain outlandish theological revelations, she promptly organized a class of peculiarly sanctified urchins whom she taught, for their special emotional edification, in the town cemetery.*

Richmond, however, instead of examining her sanity, seems, in the western manner, to have accepted her not without pride as a kind of inexplicable local genius. It disapproved of her heresies and did not sit at her feet precisely. But after all a "lady" who announced herself to be in a peculiar state of grace and sanctification could not be restrained or openly ridiculed. On a lesser and more respectable scale she was enjoying immunities similar to those which the west so chivalrously extended to "ladies" of the demi-monde who, provoked by liquor or ill temper, took strange vengeances on their admirers.

In 1890 this self-sufficient and authority-inflated matriarch brought the docile David to

---

* "The Lady with the Hatchet." By James L. Dwyer. *American Mercury*, March, 1926.

Medicine Lodge, Kansas. The region was
barely a decade away from the unfettered glories of Dodge City and Abilene, and Medicine
Lodge was but twenty miles away from the
still largely unfettered license of the Oklahoma border. The population as a whole
tended to conduct itself on the theory that
this was still cow country and man's country.
That is to say, the state prohibition law was
utterly ignored by large groups of flourishing
saloon keepers and their customers, and, although women were proportionately more
numerous than in the '70s, the principle prevailed in social codes and police policy that a
"lady" had a right to go loco whenever the
spirit moved her.

Carrie endured it ten years without any
more marked unconventionalities than a few
new theological revelations and certain mis-
sionary labors in the jail so ardent that in
the interests of the prisoners the authorities
thought it necessary to discourage them. Then
1900 came and with it the inspiration that in
a country where cowboys were still morally
entitled to shoot up saloons as a normal amusement, a lady reformer should certainly be al-

lowed to smash them up in the interests of Christian progress.

She acted upon it, first at Medicine Lodge, and then at the thriving illicit alcohol center of Kiowa on the godless Oklahoma border. No one had told her that since southern Kansas had filled up with women, their special dispensations to violence were repealed. But as a matter of fact, no one had need to. Medicine Lodge accepted the rocking of its lone pleasure palace and Kiowa the destruction of the mirrors and drinking fixtures of three, with hardly more protest than feudal villeins would have made at the rampages of a medieval duchess. Carrie had tacitly, perhaps unconsciously, assumed that she was still living in the old west of unbridled deference to feminine outbursts, and substantially Carrie was right. It was necessary for her to go to relatively urban Wichita to be arrested for her rowdiness or even to be resisted in her violence by so much as a joint-keeper's female dependents.

The rest of her career belongs to the history of moral reform and slapstick drama in America. The enormous publicity given her

Kiowa and Wichita operations raised her subsequent saloon raids somewhat above the cate-
gories of legal offenses and frontier feminist
phenomena. She was an accepted high priest-
ess now of the national cults of news interest
and the violently ludicrous. Her epic hatchet,
busy among bottles, mirrored grandeurs and
nude masterpieces, was achieving an almost
incessant series of cheerful catharses upon our
emotionally surcharged body politic. Carrie
was discharging the daily wrath of the drys
against the liquor evil, the daily suspicion of
the wets that all prohibitionists were wanton
destroyers; likewise, satisfying the lust for
laughter in those frivolous millions who pro-
fess, along with infants and cretins, that
comedy consists in doing the eccentric thing
over and over again. Thus each hatchet blow
became for millions of readers as well as for
ecstatic eye-witnesses, a purification rite. Although town marshals and sheriff's deputies,
coveting a share of her limelight, arrested her
many times, wiser judges sensed as a rule the
voters' mystical delight in her, and turned her
loose.

Symbolizing in herself and her spectacular
conduct the release of so many popular urges

From "Hard Knocks," by Col. Harry Young.

WHEN MEN WERE MEN

The Disastrous Effects of Dance-house Stimulus in Newton, Kansas, in 1867

and demi-urges, she was automatically carried onward and upward to prominence, the lecture platform and eventually into paresis. Yet, as a frontier woman exercising a frontier woman's peculiar prerogatives, she essentially created that destiny herself. . . . Or should not one say that the frontier created it for her by its astonishing fiction that a "lady," whether a strumpet in delirium tremens or a virago in a fit of moral hysteria, could do no wrong?

BRIDGET GRANT

THE excellent Mrs. Nation contributed flamboyant virtue to the cause of world progress. We come now to an equally respectable lady who utilized an equally vigorous, if somewhat different, morality to prolong a famous industrial abuse and advance the family standing.

But to leave women in their place in the home for a moment, there was a considerable row one morning in the '70s in the American consulate at Liverpool between the consul and a visitor from Portland, Oregon, who was incidentally a newspaper proprietor.

"Why," the irate official pounded on the table, "don't you people out there on the jumping-off place do something about Jim Turk and all those shanghaiers? Portland and Astoria are the worst ports in the world for this business which is a nuisance to all concerned, especially consuls. What's more, if you don't clean 'em out quick and for good, the British government's going to get busy. They're making my life miserable about it as it is.

"Why, just the other day two poor young fellows from the Coeur d'Alene were in my office telling how they'd been slugged and put aboard, and—"

"Can you find those fellows for me?" the visitor demanded, all interest.

The consul could and did. Thereby a libel suit for $50,000 brought by Jim Turk, king of the Portland sailors' boarding house keepers against Harvey W. Scott and the *Portland Oregonian* was triumphantly quashed, and a lifetime enmity was removed between Scott and the deadly editorial rival, who was the Liverpool visitor. For the two unfortunates from the Coeur d'Alene were the crux of the *Oregonian's* shanghai charges and to the *Oregonian's* lawyers their depositions were worth the weight of their physical bodies in silver.

There was, however, about these physical bodies one peculiarity which was astonishing to the point of romance, pathos, or humor according to the mood of the observers. When the young Coeur d'Aleneans dragged themselves into the consul's office a few days previously, still damp from a secretive plunge into the Mersey, these same bodies were clothed, not in conventional sailors' costume, but in vestigial chaps and other interesting fragments of cowboy gear.

Portland and Astoria were not only the worst ports in the world for a certain unpleasant sea-going labor traffic. They were the only ports in the world where cowboys were shanghaied for the vasty deep directly, as it were, off the storm decks of bucking bronchoes. They were the only ports where hands that twirled the lasso could also, under certain flagrantly compulsive conditions, be induced to manipulate the furling tackle.

But the young Coeur d'Aleneans were, to the court's satisfaction, Jim Turk's victims, and Jim Turk was not Bridget Grant. Who, then, was Bridget Grant?

If Jim Turk, a Liverpooler with fists like a battleship's broadside and the conscience of an intelligent gorilla, was king of the sailors' boarding house business, Bridget was its capitalist and the symbol of its potential respectabilities.

Born in Ireland in 1831, she had made a gloriously eugenic marriage in early life with Peter Grant, a magnificently handsome young fishing smack skipper from Prince Edward Island. He followed the cod from various

Canadian and New England ports until finally they founded in Gloucester, Massachusetts, a sailors' boarding house which promised to be more profitable than commercial adventure on the high seas. But the end of the Civil War relieved the labor shortage, always the prime point in the reckonings of boarding house keepers, and they decided to move to the Pacific coast where the shipping was enormous but men were less plentiful.

They tried it a year in San Francisco, and then came to Astoria, Oregon. Peter's fisherman's heart was undoubtedly stirred by reports of incredible salmon catches. Bridget, while open minded on the fish question, was encouraged by information that the old town at the mouth of the river was an ideal spot for craft which had been loading and recruiting crews a hundred and twenty-five miles upstream at Portland, to be caught shorthanded by reason of desertions.

But almost immediately, what should the handsome Peter do but get tangled up in his fishing gear while fooling with it within a stone's throw of his own kitchen, fall off his dock and get drowned? Bridget was forty. She had borne him nine children with such

efficient celerity that none of them was beyond
school age yet and Bridget, though illiterate
herself, had ambitious ideas about education.
But she was a fine figure of a woman, five feet
ten inches tall, perfectly proportioned, with
lustrous black hair and blue eyes, a smooth
strawberries-and-cream complexion, and strong
as a horse. Peter had left her a small sum
of cash and this brand new boarding house.
What was there to do but carry on?

Bridget did. The boarding house quickly
became famous for its immaculate cleanliness
and for setting as good a table as could be
found on any fringe of the seven seas. The
boys and girls went on with their schooling,
in wholesome frugality but without real sacrifice. While the boys were destined for the
boarding house and sailors' employment agency
business rather than for college professorships,
maternal admonition saw to it that they functioned as young intellectuals in high school.
The girls were assigned in advance to the more
refined profession of pedagogy and so were inspired to even more arduous cultural achieve-
ments. At home the indomitable matriarch
saw to the moral education, possibly utilizing
the conduct of some of the nautical guests as

sufficient evidence of the wages of iniquity. Every Grant, in any case, was taught to shun liquor and rowdy pleasures as snares of the devil, and to keep his word as his bond.

But running a successful sailors' boarding house in that time and place required something more than brilliant cookery and diligent supervision of the children's moral and intellectual progress. Portland was for all visiting sailors the acme of a long way from home. With no Panama and Suez canals to speed up ocean traffic, it was further in sailing time from New York than from Liverpool, and further from Liverpool than almost any other place to which Liverpool vessels sailed. This fact had a certain startling influence on the economics of the boarding house business.

It was generally reached after exceptionally long and confining voyages, for instance, and the new arrivals often craved exceptionally long and exceptionally thorough inebriation. While satisfying this yearning many a normally able seaman was hopelessly lost to his ship at sailing time. Also in the days of hardboiled discipline and unrestrained brutality afloat, Portland was an exceptionally tempting and advantageous town for dissatisfied but reasonably sober seamen to desert in.

Finally, a skipper himself in the bitter length of days required to make the Columbia from the Mersey or the Hudson usually had more than ample opportunity to discover whether his crew was up to standard. If it was not, if it contained an excess complement of land-lubbers, sea lawyers or of too sophisticated professional seamen, what better place could be found on any of the rims of civilization for shipping a new stock of man power and giving the undesirables the slip?

Such circumstances stimulated the labor market to an almost unprecedentedly speculative condition, and the labor market was the real basis of the sailors' boarding house industry. Whether it happened by design or accident, the skipper who had lost a whole or part of his crew was willing to pay in good clinking piles of what was familiarly called "blood money" to fill up the absentee's places with better men and true in time to work the ship down the river at something approximating the proper sailing schedule. The boarding house keepers herded the men,—it was easy, since they usually had to eat on credit,—supplied them on demand with impressive celerity, and got the "blood money" for themselves. At one time, though this is getting somewhat ahead of the story, the price per sailor, f.o.b. designated craft at a Portland wharf, was a hundred and seventy dollars.

Though smaller, Astoria was in some respects an even more profitable place for this traffic than Portland itself. For many a skipper who had recruited a crew in the metropolis discovered to his prodigious annoyance as he approached the river mouth that the majority of his prizes, scenting a penurious wage policy or careless manners with the belaying pin, had clandestinely swum ashore on the voyage down and made off to claim the hospitality of some other sailors' boarding house. With a bar to cross and already delayed in his sailing schedule by the labor difficulties of Portland, there was nothing for the irate tyrant to do but to hoist distress signals and pay such fees as the Astoria man-purveyors demanded.

Now Bridget had her boarding house in Astoria. Moreover, it was directly on the waterfront, which was unfortunate for Peter, but otherwise soundly strategic in that she could see distress signals. Indeed, a portion of it, namely the woodshed, directly overhung the water. And in the woodshed, hoisted on davits, was a Whitehall boat ready to put out at the hail of a skipper in need, with manpower enough, granted a little crowding, to see him safely to the Falkland Islands and back.

There were occasions, too, when skippers were personally and purposefully responsible for these Astoria labor emergencies. A peculiarly undesirable crew could manifest its worst qualities sometimes even in a mere hundred and twenty-five miles of river voyage, in which case means could be found of kicking it overboard at Astoria regardless of moral obligations. Or circumstances would arise which made it inauspicious for a skipper to attempt his recruiting at his official home port. There was the master, for instance, who paid his crew off at Aberdeen, Washington, a hundred miles or so up the coast on Gray's Harbor. They had proved, according to his lights, insubordinate, inefficient, useless, and therefore deserved nothing. So the captain made it his business, as each man passed before his pay window, to delay him with a tongue lashing and brawling arguments as to how much was due him, until it was quite certain that the preceding member of the riff-raff had passed down the gangplank alone. And at the foot of the gangplank stood the mate with a belaying pin, who casually knocked each man over the head as he appeared, and appropriated his wages.

Even in the era of perfect discipline it would have been inadvisable for a master to remain long in a port where he had raised such a scandal. Consequently, while his ex-crew were still stretched out in sweet vacuity on the Aberdeen dock, the captain, the mate, the cook and the captain's wife worked the ship down to Astoria, where their requirements for a crew that would put them to sea instantly, were instantly met. There is no evidence that the Widow Grant's Whitehall boat assisted in this unusual emergency. Still, the Whitehall boat was ready for all emergencies.

For a while the widow carried on alone, with the help, it seems, of a star boarder or two of the necessary athletic prowess. But in a few years her eldest sons, Jack, Peter and Ulysses, were competent to help in the labor supply operations, and shortly after came

Alexander, Ignatius and William. They all inherited the magnificent physical presence of their parents, all were six-footers and more, and all kept their word as good as their bond.

As the younger ones reached manhood and underwent their strenuous apprenticeship in the operations at Astoria, the elder sons were pushed out into the world. The world, of course, meant Portland, where Jack and Peter Grant's boarding house first at Second and D. Street, then at Third and Flanders, in the '80s took a place in fame beside the mother establishment down river. This celebrity was rapidly enhanced by the success of the Grant boys and their hard-hitting retainers in the war which Bunco Kelly, Larry Sullivan and the established masters of the metropolitan boarding house field promptly waged to prevent an invasion by talented outsiders. After a short, sharp struggle, the Grants won hands down, partly by their more powerful fists, but also by the better generalship which saw the advantages of dealing squarely with the skippers and by the better cooking which made every sailorman, no matter how unceremoniously he might find himself loaded on the deck of some hitherto unknown outgoing schooner, their friend.

Meanwhile, from Astoria, the mother managed the combat and the subsequent uncontested success with Napoleonic oversight and Napoleonic discipline. Arrangements with skippers and dealings with sailor guests were subject to her instant orders and revisions, accounts to her perpetual scrutiny. She directed the diplomatic relations with such important personages as district attorneys and competing boarding house keepers, and, on the rare occasions when it was necessary to notice them, with irate foreign consuls. Although Jack, in his maturity, conducted such subtleties in details, it was well known that the Grant politics in local and state affairs were Bridget's politics.

This iron control extended also to more personal matters. The effort of a young woman of slightly hoydenish reputation to entice Jack into matrimony in his callow years was crushed to earth by a thunderous visit from the stormy matriarch herself. One of the other sons, with advancing years and prosperity, developed an innocent fondness for toddy. But each breach of the Grant code of rigid teetotalism was reported at headquarters and he was scolded within an inch of his life for it until he was a somewhat venerable citizen himself.

When one of the daughters made an unfortunate marriage with a young Astorian rake whose strain of Italian blood was already suspect, Bridget replied to his first efforts at mistreatment by beating him up with a thoroughness which would have commended itself to a sea captain quelling a mutiny. Moreover, she arranged the divorce proceedings, paying the state Senator from Astoria in advance for his legal services and promising him,—her word was as good as her bond,—an extra twenty dollars and a quart of whiskey when the family connection with the "organ-grinding dago" of vernacular lineage had been definitely dissolved. For the Widow Grant's language in rage, it must be admitted parenthetically, was not always as correct as her morals.

Yet it was a dictatorship which proved its worth by results. The Grant boys' boarding house in Portland grew in size and patronage and the boys themselves came to exercise an authority over the whole sea-faring labor market of the metropolis comparable to that of the United States Steel chairman in the steel industry. In Astoria, Bridget also expanded until at one time or another she owned every hotel and boarding house in that most profitable of call ports. She had, too, before many years her farm on Young's River. Here in slack seasons she would send seafaring guests for a season of wholesome country life which served a quadruple economic purpose. Isolation kept them sober, and prevented their falling into the hands of rival agencies. The absence of so many sailormen from the Astoria employment lists often, in crises for skippers, would boost the "blood money" fee itself. And there was the advantage that in hard times when it was necessary to await the arrival of an uncertain next employer in order to collect a sailor's board bill, Bridget could get a little unskilled farm work out of them to make hospitality pay its overhead.

Meanwhile under the mother's direction the Grants maintained the prestige of the boarding house game by avoiding its more fatuous abuses. Portland and Astoria were never, on their own account, western towns of the wild and woolly vintage. After they passed their early and relatively quiet fur post stage, they and the surrounding countryside were settled mainly by missionaries, wheat-farmers, or-

chardists and solid merchants. There were no
disorders or peculiarly masculine hardships and
adventures to be encountered. Hence women
were brought along in normal proportions from
the beginning and western Oregon settled down
to home life varied with such strictly conventional amusements as church sociables, literary
clubs, husking bees and evening receptions.

Yet geography made both towns, especially
Portland, capitals willy nilly of a wild western
hinterland. Prospectors swarmed in the mountains, sophisticated in all the arts of open depravity that had been practiced from Sutter's
Point to Deadwood. Cowboys of Texan and
Arizonan mannerisms owned the arid plains
back of the Cascades. Lumberjacks shortly
were on hand to contribute a boisterousness
peculiarly their own. These classes descended
on Portland from time to time with the un-
spent earnings of their months of social isolation, solemnly vowed to make the staid Boston
of the north Pacific hum like a cowtown or a
mining camp. And Portland, while deprecat-
ing their revels on prayer meeting nights and
holding itself piously aloof from them, had
sufficient commercial acumen to furnish its
guests with ample facilities.

Naturally, many young roisterers who allowed the city's exhilarating night life to throw them into a state of advanced befuddlement, left it, more unconscious than ever, by way of a sailor's boarding house on the deck of some craft outward bound for almost any port between Yokohama and Lisbon. The young Coeur d'Aleneans undoubtedly belonged to this class of unfortunates. Hence, there was much indignation from time to time from ranchers and lumber bosses and occasionally from bereaved wives in the hinterland. Now and then there were even more violent explosions from skippers who had paid "blood money" for able seamen.

It was Bridget's pride, however, that the Grants scorned such outrages. She and her sons could furnish seamen of any quantity or quality desired, but landlubbers were not her commodity unless, perhaps, some skipper, aggrieved to exasperation by some recent experience with professional sea lawyers, insisted he could be satisfied with nothing less. Then, perhaps, a Grant could tell where a convenient stock of innocents might be located—though not in the Grant boarding house.

And there were other standards of trade

ethics which the Bridget notably supported.
Boarding house keepers of the thuggish strain
might play in with unscrupulous captains, and
deliver crews of dead sailors or entirely non-
existent sailors—with the understanding that
the wages of these book-keeping illusions would
be split when next the ship returned to Portland.   But Bridget saw to it that neither she
nor any of her sons took part in such chicanery.
She played fair with the financially honest captains regardless of how their wage policies or
use of the belaying pin would look in socially
minded admiralty courts.   But the crooked
skipper was as unwelcome in her parlor office
and to her sons' company as that lowest of ver-
tebrate creatures, the Swedish squarehead who
beat his board bill.

Neither, for that matter, were the Grants
graspingly mercenary.   When the hundred
and seventy dollars "blood money" fee became
a public scandal to the extent that the foreign
consuls, including the perpetually indignant
Mr. Laidlaw of her British majesty's service,
threatened to make an international issue of it,
Jack Grant calmly went before the local fact-
finding commission and agreed to reduce it to
fifty dollars.   The tactless Mr. Laidlaw replied

by insinuating that the word of "such persons" as sailors' boarding house keepers might not be reliable.

But just here Bridget had one of her great days of pride. For the company of Portland's best financial leadership and reforming talent was openly and frankly shocked. What? A Grant's word not as good as his bond? Queen Victoria's agent had practically cast a slur on Portland's civic integrity. . . . The indignant Jack, quite possibly at Bridget's suggestion, promptly played the part of dignified pathos by posting a thousand dollar bond to keep the fifty dollar pledge, although no such gesture was legally required of him.

So things went on and the sailor labor supply game which, in cruder hands, had been known as shanghaiing, became under Bridget's competent mastery a respectable profession. Moved by the rising passion for altruism, other ports other nations were legally eliminating it. But Portland and Astoria clung to their old ways, while the Grants, dealing efficaciously but honorably according to their lights, raked in the profits.

Bridget was in her sixties and then in her

seventies, but the cooking and the strategy in the big house down at the foot of Commercial Street in Astoria and in the bigger house in Portland, were as expert as ever. She was seventy-four when the final blow came and a republic, confident that it could exert a better guardianship over the business affairs of sailors than Bridget or they themselves could, put the whole employment problem in the hands of government agencies. But so far as Portland agitations were concerned, she had staved off this paternalism ten years. If Portland and Astoria had been the United States of America, she no doubt would have staved it off indefinitely.

She retired to her farm on Young's River with honors. The children whom she had entertained as a daily custom for thirty years in the boarding house kitchen, with cookies and touching exhortations to scholarship, came to see her, bringing their children and at last their grand-children. Old sailors out of luck found a haven there of incomparable free feeding and other charities too numerous and too unostentatiously done to mention. She scolded the "son who drank" for his occasional toddy. She was still scolding him when, straight as a spear and handsome as a king's mother in a Gaelic saga, she was ninety-two years old.

She died in 1923, but the newspapers had little to say about it. "She was a great lady," old water-front sophisticates evaded the bright young men of the Sunday supplements, "and a friend whom I honor. I would not be a party to anything that would make people who do not know the sea or the people of the sea, hold any thought that would belittle her."

It would truly have been a civic tragedy if the frivolous 1920s had failed to see difference between shanghaiing and Bridget Grant.

THE END

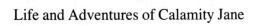

Life and Adventures of Calamity Jane

Life and Adventures
—of—
Calamity Jane,
BY HERSELF*

My maiden name was Marthy Cannary, was born in Princeton, Missourri, May 1st, 1852. Father and mother natives of Ohio. Had two brothers and three sisters, I being the oldest of the children. As a child I always had a fondness for adventure and outdoor exercise and especial fondness for horses which I began to ride at an early age and continued to do so until I became an expert rider being able to ride the most vicious and stubborn of horses, in fact the greater portion of my life in early times was spent in this manner.

In 1865 we emigrated from our homes in Missourri by the overland route to Virginia City, Montana, taking five months to make the journey. While on the way the greater portion of my time was spent in hunting along with the men and hunters of the party, in fact I was at all times with the men when there was excitement and adventure to be had. By the time we reached Virginia City I was considered a remarkable good shot and a fearless rider for a girl of my age. I remember many occurrences on the journey from Missourri to Montana. Many times in crossing the mountains the conditions of the trail were so bad that we frequently had to lower the wagons over ledges by hand with ropes for they were so rough and rugged that horses were of no use. We also had many exciting times fording streams for many of the streams in our way were noted for quicksands and boggy places, where, unless we were very careful, we would have lost horses and all. Then we had many dangers to encounter in the

*Originally appeared as a pamphlet ca. 1893.

way of streams swelling on account of heavy rains. On occasions of that kind the men would usually select the best places to cross the streams, myself on more than one occasion have mounted my pony and swam across the stream several times merely to amuse myself and have had many narrow escapes from having both myself and pony washed away to certain death, but as the pioneers of those days had plenty of courage we overcame all obstacles and reached Virginia City in safety.

Mother died at Black Foot, Montana, 1866, where we buried her. I left Montana in Spring of 1866, for Utah, arriving at Salt Lake city during the summer. Remained in Utah until 1867, where my father died, then went to Fort Bridger, Wyoming Territory, where we arrived May 1, 1868. Remained around Fort Bridges during 1868, then went to Piedmont, Wyoming, with U. P. Railway. Joined General Custer as a scout at Fort Russell, Wyoming, in 1870, and started for Arizona for the Indian Campaign. Up to this time I had always worn the costume of my sex. When I joined Custer I donned the uniform of a soldier. It was a bit awkward at first but I soon got to be perfectly at home in men's clothes.

Was in Arizona up to the winter of 1871 and during that time I had a great many adventures with the Indians, for as a scout I had a great many dangerous missions to perform and while I was in many close places always succeeded in getting away safely for by this time I was considered the most reckless and daring rider and one of the best shots in the western country.

After that campaign I returned to Fort Sanders, Wyoming, remained there until spring of 1872, when we were ordered out to the Muscle Shell or Nursey Pursey Indian outbreak. In that war Generals Custer, Miles, Terry and Crook were all engaged. This campaign lasted until fall of 1873.

It was during this campaign that I was christened Calamity Jane. It was on Goose Creek, Wyoming, where the town of Sheridan is now located. Capt. Egan was in command of the Post. We were ordered out to quell an uprising of the Indians, and were out for several days, had numerous skirmishes during which six of the soldiers were killed and several severely wounded. When on returning to the Post we were ambushed about a mile and a half from our destination. When fired upon Capt. Egan was shot. I was riding in advance and on hearing the firing turned in my saddle and saw the Captain reeling in his saddle as though about to fall. I turned my horse and galloped back with all haste to his side and got there in time to catch him as he was falling. I lifted him onto my horse in front of me and succeeded in getting him safely to the Fort. Capt. Egan on recovering, laughingly said: "I name you Calamity Jane, the heroine of the plains." I have borne that name up to the present time. We were afterwards ordered to Fort Custer, where Custer city now stands, where we arrived in the spring of 1874; remained around Fort Custer all summer and were ordered to Fort Russell in fall of 1874, where we remained until spring of 1875; was then ordered to the Black Hills to protect miners, as that country was controlled by the Sioux Indians and the government had to send the soldiers to protect the lives of the miners and settlers in that section. Remained there until fall of 1875 and wintered at Fort Laramie. In spring of 1876, we were ordered north with General Crook to join Gen'ls Miles, Terry and Custer at Big Horn river. During this march I swam the Platte river at Fort Fetterman as I was the bearer of important dispatches. I had a ninety mile ride to make, being wet and cold, I contracted a severe illness and was sent back in Gen.Crook's ambulance to Fort Fetterman where I laid in the hospital for fourteen days. When able to ride I started for Fort Laramie where I met Wm. Hickock, better known as Wild Bill, and we started for Deadwood, where we arrived about June.

During the month of June I acted as a pony express rider carrying the U.S. mail between Deadwood and Custer, a distance of fifty miles, over one of the roughest trails in the Black Hills country. As many of the riders before me had been held up and robbed of their packages, mail and money that they carried, for that was the only means of getting mail and money between these points. It was considered the most dangerous route in the Hills, but as my reputation as a rider and quick shot was well known, I was molested very little, for the toll gatherers looked on me as being a good fellow, and they knew that I never missed my mark. I made the round trip every two days which was considered pretty good riding in that country.

Remained around Deadwood all that summer visiting all the camps within an area of one hundred miles. My friend, Wild Bill, remained in Deadwood during the summer with the exception of occasional visits to the camps. On the 2nd of August, while setting at a gambling table in the Bell Union saloon, in Deadwood, he was shot in the back of the head by the notorious Jack McCall, a desperado. I was in Deadwood at the time and on hearing of the killing made my way at once to the scene of the shooting and found that my friend had been killed by McCall. I at once started to look for the assassian and found him at Shurdy's butcher shop and grabbed a meat cleaver and made him throw up his hands; through the excitement on hearing of Bill's death, having left my weapons on the post of my bed. He was then taken to a log cabin and locked up, well secured as every one thought, but he got away and was afterwards caught at Fagan's ranch on Horse Creek, on the old Cheyenne road and was then taken to Yankton, Dak., where he was tried, sentenced and hung.

I remained around Deadwood locating claims, going from camp to camp until the spring of 1877, where one morning, I saddled my horse and rode towards Crook city. I had gone about twelve miles from Deadwood, at the mouth of Whitewood creek, when I met the overland mail running from Cheyenne to Deadwood. The horses on a run, about two hundred yards from the station; upon looking closely I saw they were pursued by Indians. The horses ran to the barn as was their custom. As the horses stopped I rode along side of the coach and found the driver John Slaughter, lying face downwards in the boot of the stage, he having been shot by the Indians. When the stage got to the station the Indians hid in the bushes. I immediately removed all baggage from the coach except the mail. I then took the driver's seat and with all haste drove to Deadwood, carrying the six passengers and the dead driver.

I left Deadwood in the fall of 1877, and went to Bear Butte

Creek with the 7th Cavalry. During the fall and winter we built Fort Meade and the town of Sturgis. In 1878 I left the command and went to Rapid city and put in the year prospecting.

In 1879 I went to Fort Pierre and drove trains from Rapid city to Fort Pierce to Sturgis for Frank Witc—then drove teams from Fort Pierce to Sturgis for Fred. Evans. This teaming was done with oxen as they were better fitted for the work than horses, owing to the rough nature of the country.

In 1881 I went to Wyoming and returned in 1882 to Miles city and took up a ranch on the Yellow Stone, raising stock and cattle, also kept a way side inn, where the weary traveler could be accommodated with food, drink, or trouble if he looked for it. Left the ranch in 1883, went to California, going through the States and territories, reached Ogden the latter part of 1883, and San Francisco in 1884. Left San Francisco in the summer of 1884 for Texas, stopping at Fort Yuma, Arizona, the hottest spot in the United States. Stopping at all points of interest until I reached El Paso in the fall. While in El Paso, I met Mr. Clinton Burk, a native of Texas, who I married in August 1885. As I thought I had travelled through life long enough alone and thought it was about time to take a partner for the rest of my days. We remained in Texas leading a quiet home life until 1889. On October 28th, 1887, I became the mother of a girl baby, the very image of its father, at least that is what he said, but who has the temper of its mother.

When we left Texas we went to Boulder, Colo., where we kept a hotel until 1893, after which we travelled through Wyoming, Montana, Idaho, Washington, Oregon, then back to Montano, then to Dakato, arriving in Deadwood October 9th, 1895, after an absence of seventeen years.

My arrival in Deadwood after an absence so many years created quite an excitement among my many friends of the past, to such an extent that a vast number of the citizens who had come to Deadwood during my absence who had heard so much of Calamity Jane and her many adventures in former years were anxious to see me. Among the many whom I met were several gentlemen from eastern cities, who advised me to allow myself to be placed before the public in such a manner as to give the people of the eastern cities an opportunity of seeing the Woman Scout who was made so famous through her daring career in the West and Black Hill countries.

An agent of Kohl & Middleton, the celebrated Museum men came to Deadwood, through the solicitation of the gentleman whom I had met there and arrangements were made to place me before the public in this manner. My first engagement began at the Palace Museum, Minneapolis, January 20th, 1896, under Kohl and Middleton's management.

Hoping that this little history of my life may interest all readers, I remain as in the older days,

Yours,

Mrs. M. BURK,

BETTER KNOWN AS CALAMITY JANE